YANKEE MAGAZINE'S

More Great New England Recipes

YANKEE MAGAZINE'S

More Great New England Recipes

*And The Cooks
Who Made Them Famous*

YANKEE BOOKS

a division of
Yankee Publishing Incorporated
Dublin, New Hampshire

ACKNOWLEDGMENTS

The Editors wish to thank the following authors for use of their text material on the pages indicated: Susan Mahnke, pages 11, 21, 31, 53, 61, 71, 103, 123, 133, 141, 149, 177, 187, 199, 209, 241, 253, 265; Richard Sax, page 41; Douglas Whynott, page 79; Harriet Webster, page 87; Mel Allen, pages 97, 229; Susan DeBack, pages 113, 161; Leslie Land, pages 169, 221; and Neysa Hebbard, page 275.

The Editors also wish to thank the following photographers for use of their photographs on the pages indicated: Ulrike Welsch, pages 10, 78; Stephen O. Muskie, pages 20, 122, 140, 198; Carole Allen, pages 30, 96, 132, 252; David Witbeck, page 40; Randy O'Rourke, pages 52, 240; Mike Lafferty, page 86; W. Marc Bernsau, page 102; Paul Darling, pages 112, 176; Shelley Rotner, page 70; Nancy Nassiff, pages 60, 148, 208; Nancy Wasserman, page 160; Jeff Stevensen, pages 168, 228; Kip Brundage, pages 186, 264; Brian Vanden Brink, page 220; and Julie Houck, page 274.

Further thanks to The Countryman Press for use of recipes reprinted from *Arrowhead Farm: Three Hundred Years of New England Husbandry and Cooking* by Pauline Chase Harrell, Charlotte Moulton Chase, and Richard Chase (Woodstock, Vt.: The Countryman Press, 1983).

Book design by Jill Shaffer

Yankee Books, a division of Yankee Publishing Incorporated, Dublin, New Hampshire 03444

First Edition

Library of Congress Catalog Card No. 85-50085
ISBN: 0-89909-081-8

Contents

A Foreword

Since its beginnings in 1977, *Yankee* Magazine's "Great New England Cooks" series has drawn enthusiastic interest. "The article has gone around the world and delighted friends from Australia and Korea to Spain and Italy," one featured cook wrote. And from another came the word, "I was overwhelmed by the response . . . and also by the increase in my restaurant business." But, even in the face of such spirited response, the Yankee Books editors wondered, Would this enthusiasm hold for a collection in book form? That was in 1982; happily, the answer was yes.

The resulting collection, *Great New England Recipes and the Cooks Who Made Them Famous,* has done well. In fact, it seems there is no end to the appetite for good New England cooking and for books to share it, and praises be, it seems there is almost no end to good New England cooks to satisfy this appetite. Therefore, this "second helping" in book form from the kitchens of New England — *More Great New England Recipes,* and of course, the cooks who made them great.

This new collection is a slightly different mix. Tracing the thread of New England cooking from its very beginning some 300 years ago to a look at one of the newest wrinkles in things food, food styling, we visit a widely varied selection of cooks: some specializing in things of the sea, others in things of the land, some in the wonderful ethnic cooking that contributes so much to the area's cuisine, and some who have become expert in today's ever-more familiar haute cuisine. Then, to finish off the weave that is New England cookery, we join the cooks who engineer several of the region's most inventive gustatory entertainments — a much anticipated annual chocolate cakewalk and a close-to-community-wide holiday cookie exchange.

As with the earlier collection, the editors are indebted, first and foremost, to the more than two dozen fine New England cooks who are so generously sharing their seasoned cooking skills and superior recipes with us here. We are also deeply indebted to the Yankee Books testing kitchen network and to Karen Dionne, who somehow keeps it all in hand; to the authors and photographers who first made this splendid cookery come alive on paper; and to Martha Rice, who so carefully gathered together the necessary permissions for it all. None of this would have been possible without each of them.

Oscar Hammerstein once concluded one of his songs, "100 million miracles are happening every day." Cooking in New England (and we suppose in other corners of our world) is rather like that. Its great cooks mix ingredients, sometimes from the most unlikely places and sometimes in even the most unlikely amounts, and with care, love, and their innate skill, bring forth a minor miracle for those around them to enjoy.

We don't offer you 100 million miracle recipes here — only several hundred — but all ones we think you will enjoy!

The Editors
Yankee Books

*Polly Chase Harrell, left, and Charlotte Moulton Chase, right,
sampling their wares.*

300 Years of New England Cookery

CHARLOTTE MOULTON CHASE
and POLLY CHASE HARRELL
Newburyport, Massachusetts

Where better to begin this collection of great New England recipes than in the kitchen at Newburyport's Arrowhead Farm? There, the best of bedrock New England cooking has been practiced for a full nine generations by the descendants of William Moulton, its first settler.

In its early days, the farm, drawing on its own long list of produce — plus ample fish from the river, and spices, molasses, and tea brought almost to its doorway by visiting trading ships — was very nearly self-sufficient. Even today, the produce is still abundant enough that Charlotte Moulton Chase and her son Dick sell much of it — fresh vegetables, fruits, and flowers in season, plus honey and even Christmas trees — at their nearby Arrowhead Farm stand.

In the farm kitchen, Charlotte continues the traditional Moulton family cooking, many of the recipes drawn directly from the family's Great-Aunt Ida's now-tattered hand-scripted "receipt book." On weekends, she is often joined by her daughter, Polly Chase Harrell, who admits to "branching out" a bit on occasion. But, whether their menus are derived from the old family recipe tree or from one of its newer "branches," both cooks agree that "foods taste better at their appointed time." Thus, most of the dishes finding their way to the family's oval walnut kitchen table each mealtime are ordained by the season.

Share here in at least some of the Moulton clan's favorite recipes as the Arrowhead Farm kitchen begins its fourth century of New England cooking.

POLLY'S ZUCCHINI-CHEESE SOUP

This blend of zucchini, chicken, and cheese makes a subtly flavored luncheon soup — hot or cold.

3 to 4 pounds zucchini, sliced	2 soup cans milk
3 stalks celery, sliced	½ cup grated sharp cheddar cheese, or more to taste
5 green onions, chopped (include green parts)	Salt and freshly ground pepper to taste
2 to 3 chicken bouillon cubes	1 cup light cream
2 cans (10 ounces each) cream of chicken soup	Chopped fresh parsley, for garnish (optional)

Using a large soup pot, simmer vegetables with bouillon cubes in water just to cover. When tender, remove vegetables and purée in a blender; then return to the kettle. Add chicken soup and milk and blend thoroughly. Heat to just below boiling point. Stir in cheese, and season to taste with salt and pepper. Serve hot or cold, stirring in light cream just before serving. Garnish with chopped fresh parsley if desired. *Makes 6 generous servings.*

CORN CHOWDER

This chowder is only one of Charlotte Chase's Great-Aunt Ida's tasty recipes. Out of season, two cans (16 ounces each) of cream-style corn may be substituted for the fresh. Either way, you'll hear calls for seconds. "Common crackers" are the approximately two-inch grooved crackers so long served with chowder. After a period out of fashion, they are now being made again and are available at most "country" stores.

6 to 8 medium ears of fresh corn, shucked	5 cups milk, plus extra for soaking the crackers
5 to 6 medium potatoes, peeled and sliced	Salt and pepper to taste
1 medium onion, sliced	8 to 10 common crackers, split
4 tablespoons butter	

Cook corn in a covered kettle with a little water for about 12 minutes. Remove corn and add potatoes and onion to the corn water; cook slowly until just soft. Slice corn from cobs with a sharp knife and add to the kettle along with butter and 5 cups of the milk. Bring to a boil and simmer for 5 minutes. Salt and pepper to taste. Hold on a warm burner without further boiling for 30 to 60 minutes to gather flavor. About 25 minutes before serving, set the crackers to soak in the remaining milk (takes about 20 minutes). Then add them to the soup and serve. *Makes 8 generous servings.*

CHARLOTTE'S STUFFED EGGS

Stuffed eggs are always popular. If preparing for a crowd, you might want to triple the number of eggs and make up all three alternative additions.

8 hard-boiled eggs	Salt and pepper to taste
1 teaspoon dry mustard	Paprika and chopped
1 teaspoon vinegar	chives, for garnish
3 to 4 tablespoons	(optional)
mayonnaise	

ALTERNATE ADDITIONS:

1 medium stalk celery,	⅓ cup finely chopped
finely chopped	ham
3 slices crisp bacon,	
crumbled	

Slice hard-boiled eggs in half lengthwise. Remove yolks into a bowl and crumble with a fork. Mix dry mustard and vinegar to form a paste, then add to egg yolks along with mayonnaise, salt, and pepper. Add either celery, bacon, or ham. Stir together with a fork and mound into egg whites. If desired, garnish with a little paprika and chopped chives. *Makes 16 halves.*

SUMMER VEGETABLE SALAD
WITH COOKED DRESSING

A gaily colored and slightly sweet-sour summer salad.

6 cups coarsely chopped cold boiled new potatoes
2½ cups cold cooked peas
Salt and pepper to taste
2 tablespoons butter, melted
1½ cups cooled cooked beets, diced finer than potatoes
Cooked Salad Dressing (recipe follows)

Mix potatoes and peas together and season to taste with salt and pepper. Stir in melted butter with a fork. Add beets, stirring only until barely mixed to preserve the color appeal of the salad (beets will bleed if stirred too much). Refrigerate and serve in chilled lettuce cups with Cooked Salad Dressing.   *Serves 10 to 12.*

COOKED SALAD DRESSING

You want to use a sharp vinegar for this dressing and watch that it doesn't boil down too much.

2 cups milk
2 teaspoons prepared mustard
4 tablespoons sugar
2 tablespoons flour
2 teaspoons salt
2 eggs, beaten
½ cup cider vinegar and 4 tablespoons butter, boiled together

Scald milk in a double boiler. Mix mustard, sugar, flour, and salt thoroughly with a spoon. Stir a little of the scalded milk into this mixture, then pour back into the double boiler, stirring constantly while mixture thickens. Cook for 10 minutes. Stir in beaten eggs and cook for no more than 2 or 3 minutes. Remove from heat. Add hot vinegar and butter. Strain, cool, and store in refrigerator.

Makes approximately 2½ cups.

AUNT IDA'S WHITE BREAD

An easy-to-slice bread with a welcome old-fashioned flavor and texture. You should know that Aunt Ida's "large" spoon held approximately two of today's tablespoons.

1 large spoon sugar
2 large spoons shortening
2 cups hot milk
2 yeast cakes (or equivalent active dry yeast)
2 cups lukewarm water
3 quarts flour (about 12 cups)
1½ tablespoons salt

Dissolve sugar and shortening in hot milk, and yeast in ⅓ cup of the water. Sift flour and salt into a large bowl. Add all liquids and mix thoroughly. Turn onto a floured board and knead until smooth and elastic. Return to bowl, cover, and let rise in a warm place until doubled in bulk. Knead again, and separate into 3 large or 6 small loaves. Place each loaf in a thoroughly greased bread pan, and allow to rise again until doubled. Bake at 400°F. for 30 minutes, then reduce heat to 350° and bake until done (the loaves should sound hollow when tapped). If making the smaller loaves, bake 15 minutes at 400°, then reduce to 350° for 5 to 10 minutes more.

Makes 3 large or 6 small loaves.

BACK AND FORTH CAKES
Brown Bread Gems

Charlotte bakes these hearty molasses-flavored muffins in a rounded gem pan, which explains their name: they roll about a good bit.

½ cup rye flour	½ teaspoon salt
½ cup white flour	1 teaspoon baking soda
1 cup Indian meal	½ cup molasses
(cornmeal)	1 cup milk

Sift first 4 dry ingredients together. Dissolve baking soda in molasses; stir into dry ingredients along with milk. Pour into a greased gem pan or muffin tin. Bake at 400°F. for 20 minutes. Serve hot with butter.   *Makes 10 medium-sized muffins.*

CHARLOTTE'S BLUEBERRY MUFFINS

These nicely textured muffins are easy to prepare. At the Chases', they are frequently served with cheddar cheese omelets.

2 cups flour	1 egg, well beaten
1 tablespoon baking	1 cup milk
powder	6 tablespoons
½ teaspoon salt	shortening, melted
5 tablespoons sugar	1 cup blueberries

Sift flour, baking powder, salt, and 2 tablespoons of the sugar into a mixing bowl. Make a well in the center and add liquids — egg, milk, and melted shortening — all at once. Stir until just mixed (the mixture will still be lumpy). Add berries and stir only enough to distribute them evenly. Fill greased muffin tins two-thirds full. Sprinkle with the remaining 3 tablespoons sugar. Bake for 25 minutes at 425°F.   *Makes 12 large muffins.*

CHARLOTTE'S STRAWBERRY SHORTCAKE

A Fourth of July tradition at Arrowhead Farm. But the chopped berries are never chilled; Charlotte finds it changes their texture.

2 cups flour
4 teaspoons baking
   powder
Dash of salt
4 tablespoons butter
⅔ cup milk
1 quart strawberries,
   hulled and chopped

¾ cup sugar, mixed with
   chopped berries and
   let set at room
   temperature
1 cup heavy cream,
   whipped

Sift together flour, baking powder, and salt. Using your fingers, lightly rub butter into the flour mixture until coarse crumbs form. Gradually add milk, stirring after each addition until the dough forms a ball. Put into a lightly greased (Charlotte uses butter for flavor) shallow 9- or 10-inch cake pan, pushing the dough out to the edges. Bake at 400°F. for about 20 minutes. Remove from pan, split, butter, and cut into wedges. Add sugared strawberries and serve hot with whipped cream. If you prefer, pouring cream may be used rather than the whipped. *Makes 6 to 8 servings.*

PEACH COBBLER

This is a "peachy" change-of-pace summer dessert.

Make a shortcake mixture as outlined in Charlotte's Strawberry Shortcake recipe (above). Set aside about a third of the dough. Roll out the rest to ¼-inch thickness and line a lightly greased (again, Charlotte uses butter) rectangular 9- or 10-inch cake tin, pulling the dough up against the sides and ends of pan.

FILL WITH:

3 cups sliced fresh peaches	¾ cup sugar, sprinkled over peaches
¼ cup water	

Roll and cut remaining dough into strips and use to make a widely spaced lattice crust over the peaches. Bake at 400°F. until peaches are bubbly and crust is golden (about 25 minutes). Serve hot with pouring or whipped cream. *Ample for 9.*

PINK LEMONADE

The tartness of the lemons and sweetness of the berries will determine the amount of sugar for this refreshing sweet-sour drink.

Juice of 2 lemons	½ cup sugar, more or less to taste
1 pint strawberries or raspberries	5 cups cold water

Strain lemon juice. Mash berries and press through a sieve. Combine lemon and berry juice and stir in sugar to taste. Pour into pitcher with cold water, add plenty of ice, and head for the piazza. *With ice, serves 6.*

Kate Beattie with only one of her "upcountry" specialties.

Upcountry Cooking From Vermont

KATE BEATTIE
Danville, Vermont

More fine traditional cooking can be found farther upcountry in Danville, Vermont, in the kitchen of Kate Beattie, where Kate prepares memorable New England dishes both for her own farm family and for her daughter Marion's nearby Creamery Restaurant.

The Beattie farm, which Kate and her husband, Harold, still work, has been in the family since 1839. Its kitchen has seen a truly remarkable output of family cooking: Kate and Harold themselves have raised 14 children, many of whom still live nearby and who, with their own families, remain the focus of much of Kate's cooking. There is rarely a Beattie supper that doesn't see eight to ten at table, a number which, by dinnertime on Sunday, almost always grows to twenty or thirty.

Although Kate is widely known for her chicken pie (one without vegetables), most of her recipes extoll the goodness of Vermont maple and dairy products or her favorite local butternuts. In her hands, maple syrup finds its way into pies, onto buns, over apples and even her homemade doughnuts, and is often used in place of brown sugar. The dairy products find their way into almost everything; the butternuts into a pecanlike pie and into the cake you'll find here.

Even though Kate's incredible culinary production includes up to 300 quarts of pickles, 56 quarts of tomatoes, and 12 gallons

21

of relish each summer, she only measures when she's making a cake, which explains, she says, why "it's hard for me to give my recipes." She did, however, write out those that follow: consider yourself lucky.

MARION'S TOMATO BISQUE

This delicate blend of vegetable flavors is a delightful surprise — and easy to prepare. If fresh tomatoes are used, skin them and cook briefly to soften.

1 large onion, diced	2 quarts fresh or canned
5 or 6 ribs celery with	tomatoes, crushed
leaves, diced	2 teaspoons baking soda
2 cups fresh	3 cups heavy cream
mushrooms, diced	3 cups milk
2 green peppers, diced	Salt, pepper, garlic,
2 tablespoons plus ¼	parsley, and basil to
cup butter	taste
¼ cup cooking sherry	

In a large pot, simmer onion, celery, mushrooms, and peppers in 2 tablespoons butter and sherry until tender. Stir in tomatoes and baking soda. (The soda will prevent the cream from "wheying," or curdling.) Add cream, milk, remaining ¼ cup butter, and seasonings, and cook over low heat (do not boil) for 30 minutes. Serve very hot. The bisque can be held over a pan of boiling water if you aren't able to watch it. *Serves 6 to 8.*

CHICKEN PIE

This is the traditional no-vegetable chicken pie that Kate — and many others — prefer.

1 large stewing chicken	½ teaspoon baking soda
1 stalk celery	1 tablespoon sugar
Salt and pepper to taste	1 teaspoon salt
2 cups flour, plus extra to make the gravy	⅔ cup shortening (half butter, half Crisco)
4 teaspoons baking powder	½ cup milk (approximately)

Simmer the chicken in a large kettle with celery and salt and pepper to taste. When chicken is tender, remove it from the broth. Save the broth, discarding the celery stalk. Bone the chicken and separate into medium-sized pieces; put the pieces in the bottom of a large casserole dish. Using extra flour to thicken the reserved broth, make about a quart of gravy; while still hot, pour enough gravy over the chicken to cover. Combine the remaining 2 cups of flour, baking powder, baking soda, sugar, and salt in a bowl. Cut in the shortening and add enough milk to make a soft biscuit dough. Roll out the dough and place it over the chicken and gravy. Cut a hole in the center of the dough and insert an inverted custard cup, pressing it down into the pie (this will vent the pie and help it cook evenly). Place the pie in a preheated 425°F. oven; immediately turn heat down to 350° and bake for 45 to 50 minutes, until biscuit is golden. Serve with extra gravy nearby.   *Makes 6 to 8 helpings.*

YORKSHIRE PUDDING FOR A CROWD

Kate serves this Yorkshire Pudding with her husband's favorite birthday dinner. She makes it while the beef is roasting.

10 eggs	1 quart milk
2 tablespoons beef fat, melted (from roast beef)	4 cups flour
	2 teaspoons salt

Beat the eggs well, until completely blended. Add melted beef fat. Add milk, flour, and salt, and beat together. Let stand for about 1 hour. Pour into a buttered 12- by 16-inch roasting pan and bake about 1 hour at 375°F., or until pudding is puffed and browned. Serve at once. Note: This recipe can be halved and made in an iron skillet. *Makes 12 or more generous wedges.*

BAKED TOMATO CASSEROLE

The Beattie family is not keen on casserole cookery, but they do like this one — and, of course, it's an excellent way to help use up Kate's mammoth stock of "put by" tomatoes.

Sauté a mixture of onions, mushrooms, and celery (about 2 cups in all) in butter until tender but not browned. Add 1 quart jar canned whole tomatoes and mix together. Season as desired (basil and oregano work well, and a spoonful of sugar helps bring out the flavor). Place mixture in a 1½- to 2-quart baking dish. Cover tomato mixture with triangles of white bread, buttered well on both sides. Sprinkle with grated Parmesan cheese. Bake at 350°F. until golden. Note: Fresh tomatoes may be used, but first skin them and cook briefly to soften. *Serves 4 to 6.*

WHITE BREAD

Kate doesn't measure her bread flour precisely because, as she says, the mix varies with the weather and whether a soft or firm dough is wanted. However, she does have two favorite flours — King Arthur and Robin Hood.

2 packages (scant tablespoon each) active dry yeast, dissolved in a little warm water
1 quart milk
¾ cup shortening (half butter, half Crisco)

3 eggs
¾ cup sugar
2 teaspoons salt
8 to 10 cups flour
Butter, for topping

Dissolve yeast in warm (105° to 115°F.) water. Meanwhile, heat milk gently and dissolve the butter and Crisco in the warm milk. Let milk cool to lukewarm. Beat in eggs and sugar. Combine the yeast mixture with the milk mixture; add salt and enough flour to make a bread dough that is easy to handle. Knead well. Let dough rise in a large greased bowl or kettle in a warm place until doubled. Punch down and shape into loaves as desired. Let rise in greased pans until doubled and bake at 350°F. for 30 to 40 minutes or until bread sounds hollow when tapped. Grease the tops with butter while still hot. This makes the crusts soft and shiny.

Makes 4 or 5 medium-sized loaves or 3 large.

MAPLE STICKY BUNS: Let dough rise once, then roll out a portion of dough into a large rectangle. Spread with butter and maple syrup and roll up. Cut into ½-inch slices and place slices flat in a large baking dish. Let rise, then pour on more maple syrup (½ to ⅔ cup) and bake at 350°F. until done (about 25 to 30 minutes). Serve hot. *Makes about 2 dozen.*

BREAD AND BUTTER PICKLES

An excellent and simple pickle to make, and only one of the many Kate "puts up" each year.

6 quarts thinly sliced,
   well-scrubbed,
   unpeeled cucumbers
1 quart thinly sliced
   small onions
½ cup pickling salt
3 cups pure cider
   vinegar

6 cups sugar
¼ cup mustard seed
2 tablespoons whole
   cloves
1 tablespoon celery seed
1 teaspoon turmeric
   (optional)

Combine sliced cucumbers and onions in a large shallow pan. Sprinkle pickling salt over all and mix in with your hands. Cover with ice and let sit for 3 hours or more. Drain. Rinse in cold water. Drain again thoroughly.

Make a brine of vinegar, sugar, and spices and bring to a boil. Add drained vegetables and bring to a boil again for 3 to 4 minutes. Pack in hot sterilized jars and seal immediately.

Yield: 5 to 6 quarts.

KATE'S DOUGHNUTS

*Kate offers these tasty doughnuts with maple syrup for dunking. She
always uses sour milk or buttermilk — never sweet.*

2 cups sour milk or
  buttermilk
½ stick (¼ cup) butter,
  melted
2 cups sugar
3 eggs plus 2 egg yolks
2 teaspoons baking soda
2 teaspoons baking
  powder
½ teaspoon salt
2 teaspoons nutmeg
Enough flour to make a
  soft dough (5 or 6
  cups)
Oil or melted lard, for
  frying

Combine sour milk, melted butter, sugar, and eggs, and stir until
smooth. Sift dry ingredients together. Combine wet and dry ingredients, adding enough flour to make a dough that is easy to handle,
but not too stiff. Do not overmix, or dough will be tough. Roll out
dough to about ½-inch thickness and cut with a doughnut cutter.
Fry in hot (370°F.) melted lard or oil. (Kate uses an 8-inch kettle
about two-thirds full of oil and watches to be sure the oil doesn't
get *too* hot.)   *Makes 4 to 5 dozen.*

BUTTERNUT CAKE

This fabulous cake calls for a rather unique technique that results in a texture somewhere between "sponge" and "pound."

2 eggs, well beaten	¼ cup butter
2 cups sugar	Vanilla, lemon, or
2 teaspoons baking	almond flavoring
powder	(about 1 teaspoonful)
2 cups all-purpose flour	Maple Butternut
Dash of salt	Frosting (recipe
1 cup milk	follows)

Beat eggs and sugar together. Combine dry ingredients and add to egg mixture. Bring milk and butter just to a boil and pour over cake mixture. Beat well. Add flavoring as desired. Pour into a 9- by 13-inch greased and floured pan and bake at 350°F. for about 30 to 40 minutes or until cake tests done. Frost with Maple Butternut Frosting. *Makes 12 or more servings.*

MAPLE BUTTERNUT FROSTING

Kate prefers Grade B syrup for her maple cookery; she finds it gives more flavor.

1⅔ cups Grade B maple	1 cup butternuts
syrup	(walnuts may be
2 egg whites, beaten stiff	substituted)

Cook syrup until it spins a long thread (238° to 240°F.). (When heating syrup, be careful that it doesn't boil over; if it does, add a bit of butter, cream, or a piece of salt pork to bring it down.) Pour hot syrup over beaten egg whites, and beat until frosting has lost its gloss. Spread over cake. Top with butternuts.

MAPLE CREAM PIE

This is the pie that gets never-fail raves at Marion Beattie's Creamery Restaurant. Kate cooks the custard thoroughly to eliminate any raw taste from the flour.

2¼ cups milk	A 10-inch pie shell,
2 cups Grade B maple	baked (see following
syrup	recipe)
3 egg yolks, well beaten	1 cup heavy cream,
4 heaping tablespoons	whipped, with sugar
flour	and vanilla (optional)
Dash of salt	added to taste
2 teaspoons vanilla	

Combine milk, syrup, egg yolks, and flour in a double boiler. Cook slowly over simmering water for about 30 minutes. Add salt. Remove from heat and stir in vanilla. Pour into baked pie shell (use Kate's Pie Crust or your own favorite) and chill until firm. Top chilled pie with whipped cream just before serving. Note: Any extra custard may be used as a pudding, but be sure to keep refrigerated. *Pie makes 8 generous pieces.*

KATE'S PIE CRUST

Kate warns new pie bakers to be on guard against adding too much ice water. Wet pie crust dough is useless.

6 cups flour	2 to 2½ cups lard
⅔ cup sugar	(approximately)
2 teaspoons salt	Ice water

In a large bowl, combine flour, sugar, and salt. Work in lard by hand, adding enough so that mixture is crumbly and coarse. At this point, mixture can be refrigerated. To complete the crust, take out as much as needed (approximately 2 cups of the mixture for a double-crust pie) and add just enough ice water to form the dough into a ball without making it sticky. Roll out crusts and fill pie as desired. *Ample for three double-crust pies.*

Emma Tourangeau away from her kitchen.

Culinary Heirlooms à la Française

EMMA TOURANGEAU
Portland, Maine

Many threads go to make the weave of traditional New England cookery, not the least of them the *tambour* (winter cupboard), rich with classic French-Canadian dishes brought south to New England by immigrants from Quebec and other French towns north of the St. Lawrence. Emma Mailly and Ludger Tourangeau, mother and father of Emma, were two such immigrants. They brought their French-Canadian recipes from Quebec — "my family heirlooms," Emma calls them — to Westbrook, Maine, where Emma was born on December 14, 1884, just over 100 years ago.

Aunt Emma, as almost everyone greets her, still vividly recalls a childhood full with French-Canadian customs, many revolving around mealtimes and the food served; for Sunday dinner, roasted pork with *pommes de terre à la Rose,* turnips, pickled beets, French bread from her grandfather's bakery, and always a surprise pie in season. The very special *tourtière* (pork pie) was reserved for Christmas and New Year's Eve, when it would be "served with applesauce or with apple rings fried in butter."

In the 1940s, Emma and her sister Virginia bought a cottage on Peaks Island ("If you haven't lived on an island," Emma scolds, "you haven't lived"), Emma commuting each weekday to her bookkeeping job in Portland — a job she held for 46 years. On the island, Emma broadened her cooking interests to include the local seafood ("If we had eggs and cream and fresh fish, we could make an elegant meal") and published her popular *Aunt Emma's Island Cookbook* (now out of print but still in demand).

Today, Emma Tourangeau makes her home at a nursing home in Portland, where she is busily updating her cookbook and working on her family memoirs; as she puts it, getting "the memories that cling to me" down. And until very recently, Emma could still be found preparing the traditional *tourtière* and *pâté au saumon* (salmon pie) — only two of the "family heirlooms" she shares with you here.

SOUPE AUX POIS
Pea Soup

For this delicious, hearty soup you may use either split (yellow) or whole (green) peas. However, the French Canadian prefers the yellow.

In a large soup kettle, soak 1 pound of split (yellow) or whole (green) peas for about 10 hours, or overnight. Rinse the soaked peas; drain; bring them to a boil with 3 quarts cold water and ½ pound salt pork. The pork may be cut up, but it is traditional to leave it in a chunk. Add 1 medium onion (peeled), and a clove or two of garlic (garlic is optional). Some cooks add finely diced carrots, turnips, and a little bay leaf, but the traditional soup contains just the peas, pork, and onion. Simmer the soup, covered, for 2 or 3 hours, until the peas have completely disintegrated. Season to taste and serve. Note: If you add bay leaf, it's best to remove it before serving. *Makes 6 generous cupfuls.*

LA TOURTIÈRE
Pork Pie

You may use either the Pie Crust for Two (Two-Crust) Pies or the more unusual Bride's Pie Crust, or your own favorite, for this traditional French-Canadian holiday dish. Emma's father preferred his tourtière *without potatoes, so she always made two.*

1 (4-pound) pork butt, boned and ground (save the bones)	½ teaspoon pepper
	4 medium potatoes
1 quart salted water	Pastry for 2 double-crust pies (not too rich)
2 medium onions, finely chopped	
2 tablespoons butter	Cracker or dried bread crumbs as needed
1 teaspoon salt	

Choose a pork butt that is as lean as possible. Boil the bones in 1 quart of boiling salted water for about 20 minutes; remove the bones and set the liquid aside. In a large heavy kettle, sauté onions in butter until golden brown. Add ground pork and a cup or so of the bone broth. Then add salt and pepper, and simmer for 1½ to 2 hours. Simmer as slowly as possible, continuing to add more of the bone "liquor" to prevent scorching. The pork should be well cooked and lose all its pink color. Meanwhile, boil and mash the potatoes, adding a little salt, pepper, and butter. Drain and cool the pork and onion mixture and combine it with the mashed potatoes. Divide the mixture evenly in 2 unbaked pie shells. Before putting on the top crusts, sprinkle on just a few very fine cracker or bread crumbs to help absorb some of the fat. Bake at 400°F. for 10 minutes; reduce heat and bake at 350° for 30 minutes longer or until nicely browned. These pies can also be frozen unbaked, and then baked (unthawed) at 350° for an hour or until browned. Serve with Emma's Harvard Beets and/or applesauce. Note: Some French Canadians prefer a spicier *tourtière,* adding perhaps 1 teaspoon cinnamon and ½ teaspoon each of ground nutmeg and cloves for each 2-pie recipe.   *Makes 2 pies; 12 generous servings.*

PIE CRUST FOR TWO (TWO-CRUST) PIES

This is a superior pie crust that is both flaky and tender yet holds its shape very well.

1½ cups lard or shortening	2 teaspoons salt
	½ cup boiling water
2 tablespoons milk	4 cups flour

Place shortening, milk, and salt in a bowl. Pour on the boiling water and whip with a fork or beater until the consistency of whipped cream. Stir in flour; finish blending using your fingers. Shape into a ball and cool thoroughly (at least 2 hours) before rolling out. *Makes more than enough for 2 double-crust 9-inch pies.*

BRIDE'S PIE CRUST

This more unusual recipe is easy to prepare and makes a lovely crust. But allow ample time to chill — two hours or more.

2 cups Crisco	1 cup ginger ale
4 cups flour	½ teaspoon salt

Blend shortening and flour. Add ginger ale and salt. Mix thoroughly with hands. Chill well and roll out.

Enough for 2 double-crust 8-inch pies.

PÂTÉ AU SAUMON
Salmon Pie

This tasty stick-to-your-ribs pie makes an excellent luncheon or supper dish, though in French Canada it is sometimes served for breakfast.

2 medium potatoes,
  peeled and cubed
1 medium onion,
  chopped very fine
4 tablespoons butter
1 large can (15 ounces)
  red salmon, cleaned
  of skin and bones

3 to 4 tablespoons hot
  milk, plus extra for
  brushing crust
Salt and pepper to taste
Pastry for a 9-inch pie
Paprika (optional)

Cook potatoes and onion together until tender; drain and mash, adding butter and mixing until smooth. Combine salmon with the potato mixture; add hot milk, and salt and pepper to taste. Spoon onto bottom crust; add top crust and seal. Brush top crust with a little milk, and sprinkle with paprika if desired. Bake at 400°F. for 10 minutes; reduce heat to 350° and bake 45 minutes longer.

Ample for a 9-inch pie to serve 8.

100-YEAR-OLD PIE CRUST

Another excellent and easy-to-handle pie crust.

2½ cups flour
1 cup lard (no
  substitutes)

Dash of salt
1 tablespoon vinegar
½ cup milk

Combine flour and lard and mix well with a pastry blender or two knives. Add salt and vinegar to milk and stir. Then combine milk mixture with flour and lard. Blend; shape into a ball and chill for 2 hours. Roll out on a floured pastry board.

Makes ample for a double-crust 8-inch pie.

MOLDED CHICKEN SALAD

This makes an excellent luncheon dish as is, or you can play with it a bit. Add whatever you like, as long as it isn't watery.

3 chicken legs
3 chicken breasts
2½ quarts plus ¾ cup water
2 large onions
1 large stalk celery, plus 1 cup finely chopped
1 tablespoon salt
1 envelope (1 tablespoon) Knox unflavored gelatin
¾ cup mayonnaise
2 cups mixed chopped vegetables: green peppers, stuffed olives, carrots, small amount of pimiento
Salt and pepper to taste
1 can (15 ounces) pineapple chunks, drained
¼ cup chopped pecans
Sliced stuffed olives (optional)

Boil chicken legs and breasts in 2½ quarts water with onions, celery stalk, and salt. Simmer slowly for 1½ hours. Cool in broth. Put ¾ cup water in a small pan; sprinkle in gelatin and stir over low heat until just dissolved. Cool for 30 minutes. Stir mayonnaise into gelatin. Blend well and set aside. Remove chicken from broth; bone to get about 2 cups of meat (equal portions of light and dark). Add chopped celery and mixed vegetables. Combine chicken, vegetables, and mayonnaise mixture thoroughly. Add salt and pepper to taste. Stir in drained pineapple and pecans. Wet a 2-quart mold. If desired, arrange sliced stuffed olives on the bottom to make a pattern when the aspic is inverted. Spoon in the chicken mixture carefully and chill until firm. Unmold and serve.

Makes 6 ample servings.

EMMA'S HARVARD BEETS

These sweet-sour beets have a beautiful, bright color and a lovely smooth sauce that doesn't turn gummy.

3 cups freshly cooked boiled beets (or use canned)	½ cup vinegar
	1 tablespoon cornstarch
	2 whole cloves
½ cup sugar	2 tablespoons butter
½ teaspoon salt	

Slice or dice the beets. In a double boiler, combine sugar, salt, vinegar, cornstarch, and cloves. Cook the sauce until it is clear. Add the beets and heat over hot water for 30 minutes — do not boil. Remove cloves and then add butter just before serving.

Serves 6 to 8.

RHUBARB PUDDING
An Old Recipe

This unique pudding is guaranteed to draw raves from rhubarb lovers.

1 quart rhubarb, cut up	1 cup flour
1½ cups sugar	1 teaspoon baking powder
¼ cup butter, melted	¼ teaspoon salt
1 teaspoon vanilla	
2 eggs, well beaten	

Mix rhubarb and 1 cup sugar. Place in a buttered 2-quart baking dish. Combine melted butter, vanilla, eggs, flour, baking powder, remaining ½ cup sugar, and salt; pour over rhubarb. Bake at 375°F. for 45 minutes or until done: the pudding will be a bit soft inside. Good served warm with maple syrup.   *Serves 6 to 8.*

DESSERT AU RIZ
A Very Old Recipe

This delicious rice dessert is served either warm or cold with fruit, and is especially good with blueberries and a sprinkling of cinnamon.

½ cup raisins	¼ teaspoon salt
2 cups milk	Vanilla or lemon juice
2 cups cooked rice	(½ teaspoon or to
2 eggs, separated	taste)
½ cup brown sugar	

Soak raisins in hot water to cover until raisins are soft. In a double boiler, heat milk and rice. Beat egg yolks until smooth, then add brown sugar and salt. Add milk and rice mixture very slowly, then pour back into the double boiler and cook over boiling water until very thick. Fold in beaten egg whites. Add vanilla or lemon juice; fold in drained raisins. *Makes about 4 cups.*

VARIATION: This pudding can be cooked with a meringue top. Proceed as above; do not fold in egg whites. Instead, preheat the oven to 425°F. and pour the cooked pudding into a 2-quart baking dish. Beat the egg whites with 2 tablespoons powdered sugar and ½ teaspoon lemon juice. Spoon meringue over the pudding and bake for 5 minutes or until brown. Serve within 1 hour.

Serves 4 to 6.

BANANA PUDDING

This rich pudding is good warm or cold.

1 cup flour	1 teaspoon vanilla
4 egg yolks	1 package vanilla wafers
½ cup sugar	Several (3 or 4) bananas,
1 quart milk	thinly sliced

In a saucepan, combine flour, egg yolks, sugar, and milk. Mix until smooth. Bring slowly to a boil and cook until thick and the consistency of pudding. Stir in vanilla. In a 2-quart casserole dish, place a layer of vanilla wafers, a layer of thinly sliced bananas, and about half of the pudding. Repeat, working quickly because the heat of the pudding turns this into a cakelike mixture. *Serves 6 to 8.*

Mary Codola getting ready for Christmas Eve.

Italian Christmas Eve *Festa*

MARY CODOLA
Barrington, Rhode Island

Just as French-Canadian recipes have joined those of the original colonial settlers to make up the New England cookery we all know today, so have those of the many Italian immigrants — early and late — who came to New England to make their homes.

Nowadays, most Italian-American cooking blends, as do many Italian-American families, the food and customs of several different Italian regions. This is certainly true of the Codola family: Mary's mother is from Scafati, near Naples, while her husband Pat's mother came from Atrani, a tiny seacoast village — each town having its own distinct cuisine. The menu that Mary invites us to share reflects this. It is the one reserved for the family's annual Christmas Eve feast, and more nearly resembles the holiday dinner served for many years by her mother-in-law, rather than the one Mary knew as a girl.

Traditionally, the Italian Christmas Eve dinner is meatless, and many families still observe the time-honored ritual of offering 13 separate fish dishes (to represent Christ and each of the 12 disciples). Mary usually limits her holiday fish dishes to five (baked stuffed shrimp, clams casino, a codfish salad, a snail salad, and fried smelts). To these she adds a nontraditional escarole (*scarola*) soup with meatballs, a pasta with red clam sauce, kale, Italian bread, and an assortment of sweets. Recipes for most of these follow, along with a *polpettone*, one of Mary's many specialties not reserved for holiday time. *Buono appetito!*

41

ESCAROLE SOUP WITH TINY MEATBALLS

Optional additions to this "sign of forgiveness" soup are sliced hard-boiled eggs and freshly grated Parmesan cheese.

1 fowl (about 5 to 6 pounds)	1 bay leaf
2 meaty beef shank bones (1½ to 2 pounds)	6 peppercorns
	Salt to taste
	1 to 1½ cups escarole
2 medium onions, peeled and quartered	½ cup uncooked small pasta (e.g., tiny shells, orzo, or acini di pepe)
2 carrots, coarsely chopped	½ pound ground chuck
1 rib celery, coarsely chopped	Freshly ground pepper to taste
1 leek, trimmed, cleaned, and coarsely chopped	

In a large stockpot or kettle, place the fowl (including all giblets except the liver) and the beef bones. Add enough cold water to cover generously and bring slowly to a boil, partially covered. Skim off all froth; lower heat to a simmer. Add onions, carrots, celery, leek, bay leaf, and peppercorns, and salt to taste. Simmer, partially covered, until fowl is tender. Remove fowl and continue to simmer until beef is very tender. Remove beef shank bones. When cool enough to handle, trim meat from bones; set meat aside, return bones to pot, and continue to simmer another 1 to 2 hours or until broth is nicely flavored.

Degrease the broth, then strain, thoroughly cool, and chill (this can be done in advance and the broth refrigerated). While broth is chilling, be sure both stewed fowl and beef are properly stored. The next day, lift off fat from the broth, leaving a few small pieces on the surface for flavor. Cut beef and 2 or more cups, as desired, of the chicken into bite-sized pieces (reserve remaining chicken for another use). Set both the chicken and beef aside, covered and refrigerated.

As mealtime approaches, cook escarole, uncovered, in salted water to cover until just tender — about 15 minutes. Drain, rinse under cold water, drain well, and cut in bite-sized pieces. Set aside. (If you prefer, escarole may be cooked ahead and frozen. In that case, add just before serving, allowing ample time for it to heat through.) In a separate pan of boiling water, cook pasta until *al dente* (firm-tender); drain, rinse under cold water, drain well, and set aside.

Season ground chuck with a little salt and freshly ground pepper and roll into tiny ½-inch meatballs. Set aside on a plate, covered and refrigerated.

At serving time, bring broth to a boil and correct seasonings. Drop in meatballs and simmer briefly, until just cooked through. Add reserved beef, chicken, escarole, and pasta and stir. Serve hot.   *Ample for 12.*

KALE WITH LEMON AND GARLIC

To preserve the flavor and vitamin content, cook the kale as quickly as possible and drain immediately.

3 to 4 pounds fresh kale	Salt to taste
Olive oil	Lemon wedges
2 to 3 cloves garlic,	
minced or crushed	

Clean kale thoroughly, rinsing the leaves in several changes of cold running water. Strip leaves off stalks; discard stalks. Boil leaves, uncovered, in salted water to cover. Cook just until tender (20 to 25 minutes) and drain well in a colander. Transfer to a serving dish or mixing bowl. Drizzle on enough olive oil to coat, tossing leaves gently. Add garlic and salt to taste. Serve hot or cold with lemon wedges on the side.   *Serves 6 to 8.*

LINGUINE ALLE VONGOLE
Linguine with Red Clam Sauce

Italian red clam sauce is made differently than the white clam sauce many know. It contains no butter or cheese.

2 tablespoons olive oil	Bottled clam juice, if
4 to 5 whole cloves	needed
garlic	2 pounds linguine
2 cans (1 pound 12	Hot red pepper flakes
ounces each) crushed	(about ½ teaspoon)
tomatoes	Salt to taste
⅓ cup dry red wine	Chopped fresh parsley
1 quart fresh shelled	
clams, with their	
liquid (about 4 quarts	
in the shell)	

In a large saucepan, heat olive oil and sauté garlic until lightly golden. Add tomatoes and wine and bring to a boil, stirring. Drain clams and add their liquid to pan. Simmer uncovered, stirring often, for 1½ hours. If necessary, add bottled clam juice to give a good seafood flavor.

Clean clams. If clams are large, remove bellies. Chop clams coarsely and add to warm sauce just before serving time, letting them simmer 10 minutes or so.

Cook linguine until *al dente*. Place pasta in shallow serving dish or individual bowls. Season sauce with red pepper flakes and salt to taste. Pour sauce over pasta and sprinkle with chopped parsley. *Serves 8.*

BACCALA INSALATA
Salt Codfish Salad

Flecked with red and green, and topped with lemon slices, this makes an attractive main-dish salad as well as a tasty one.

1½ to 2 pounds dried salt cod	Chopped fresh parsley
Olive oil	Hot red pepper flakes
Fresh lemon juice	Lettuce leaves and lemon slices, for garnish
Finely minced or crushed garlic	

Soak dried salt cod in a large pan of cold water for 1 to 3 days, until tender. Change the water every day (sometimes salt cod is available presoaked or partially soaked; if so, it needs less soaking time).

When cod is moist and tender, drain well and place in a saucepan with water to cover. Bring to a boil, lower heat, and simmer just until fish flakes with a fork. Do not overcook (10 minutes is usually enough). Drain fish well and cool.

Separate cod into large flakes, working gently with your fingers. Transfer to a mixing bowl. Add the dressing as you would to a salad, adding ingredients to suit your preference. First, pour on enough olive oil to coat the fish generously. Then add fresh lemon juice and garlic to taste, and sprinkle on plenty of parsley and red pepper, tossing gently. The cod should be flecked with lots of red and green. Put in a serving dish and garnish with lettuce leaves and lemon slices. *Serves 6 or more.*

POLPETTONE
Stuffed Meat Roll

Not being meatless, polpettone would not be on the menu at a "proper" Italian Christmas Eve feast. There are a number of ways to make this fine dish, but Mary's, when sliced, reveals a cross section of hard-boiled egg. This recipe is enough to make two rolls.

MEAT ROLL:

6 eggs
1½ cups stale Italian bread without crusts, crumbled
Warm water (about 3½ cups)
2 pounds ground beef
1 teaspoon salt
1 teaspoon freshly ground black pepper
3 cloves garlic, minced
⅓ cup freshly chopped parsley
1 cup freshly grated Parmesan cheese
Milk, if needed
2 tablespoons olive oil
2 cloves garlic, bruised but left whole

SAUCE:

2 cans (1 pound 12 ounces each) crushed tomatoes
1 cup water
¼ cup dry red wine, or as needed
3 tablespoons freshly chopped parsley
Salt and freshly ground black pepper to taste

VEGETABLE GARNISH:

1½ tablespoons olive oil
1 medium onion, cut into thin slivers
2 packages (10 ounces each) frozen tiny peas, partially thawed

To Make the Meat Rolls: Hard-boil 4 of the eggs and set them aside to cool. In a bowl, combine the crumbled bread with enough warm water to cover (about 3½ cups), and set aside until the bread has softened (about 5 minutes). Squeeze the bread dry, crumbling it, and place it in a large mixing bowl with the meat. Lightly beat the remaining 2 eggs and add them to the meat mixture along with the salt, pepper, garlic, parsley, and Parmesan cheese. Combine the ingredients thoroughly, using a light touch. The mixture should be quite moist and somewhat pasty, though not wet. If it is too dry, add a splash of milk. Lay about one-fourth of the meat mixture on a waxed paper-covered platter or tray, forming it into a cylindrical shape about 6 inches long. With the side of your hand, form a deep trough down the center of the cylinder. Shell the hard-boiled eggs and trim off the small end of each. Lay 2 of the eggs, end to end, down the center of the roll. Carefully pack another fourth of the remaining meat mixture around the eggs, forming a neat, smooth cylinder. (Be sure that the roll is not too long to fit in the pot you intend to simmer it in.) Repeat the process for the second roll. Chill the rolls until firm, at least an hour.

In a large skillet, heat the olive oil, then simmer the bruised garlic for a few minutes, until lightly golden. Discard the garlic. Smooth the meat rolls again to be sure they are even, then brown them in the skillet over medium heat until deep brown on all sides. Work carefully with two spatulas to avoid breaking the rolls.

To Add the Sauce: Carefully transfer both browned *polpettone* to a deep pot, then cover with the tomatoes and the water. Bring the mixture to a very slow simmer, and simmer, uncovered, 1½ hours. The rolls should be nearly submerged; spoon the sauce over them if they are not covered. Stir the sauce carefully from time to time, degreasing it occasionally as needed. Add the wine and simmer the sauce until it is quite thick and the rolls are firm — about another 20 minutes. Carefully remove the meat rolls to a platter, and cool, if you have time. Then add the parsley and necessary seasonings.

To Add Vegetable Garnish: While the meat and sauce are simmering together, heat the oil in a saucepan and cook the onion until lightly golden. Meanwhile, boil the peas in a large pot of boiling salted water until just tender — 5 minutes or less. Drain the peas and add to the onion. Toss together gently and keep warm.

To Serve: Carefully slice the *polpettone,* using a large serrated knife. Arrange the slices on a large heated platter, overlapping them slightly. Scatter the vegetable mixture around the slices. Serve the sauce separately with macaroni on the side.   *Serves 10 to 12.*

MINIATURE CANNOLI
Cream-filled Pastries

These elegant pastries are time-consuming to prepare but oh, so good! You'll need cannoli forms for this recipe. They are metal tubes about 5¾ inches long by an inch in diameter.

CANNOLI DOUGH:

1½ cups all-purpose flour
¾ cup solid vegetable shortening, chilled
1½ tablespoons sugar
3 ounces cold water, or as needed

3 ounces milk, or as needed
Crisco oil, for deep-frying

CREAM FILLING:

⅔ cup flour
⅔ cup sugar
Pinch of salt
3 cups cold milk
4 egg yolks, lightly beaten

4 tablespoons unsalted butter, cut up
2 teaspoons vanilla

GARNISH:

30 maraschino cherries, halved

Shredded coconut (½ to ¾ cup)
Confectioners' sugar

To Make Dough: In a mixing bowl or food processor, cut together flour, shortening, and sugar until mixture is crumbly. In a small cup, stir together water and milk; then add just enough of the liquid mixture to form a soft, but not wet, dough. On a lightly floured surface, roll dough out very thin (no more than ⅛-inch thick). Cut with a serrated pizza cutter or a knife into 2½- by 3-inch rectangles.

To Fry Dough: Heat oil in a large pan until hot but not smoking (a small piece of dough should sizzle gently when placed in the oil). Wrap each rectangle of dough around the metal *cannoli* forms, placing one corner of the dough in the center of the tube, moistening it with cold water or beaten egg white, and bringing opposite corner up and over to seal. Gently hold the corners of the dough together with tongs and immerse the dough in oil, holding until the corners seal (a few seconds). Fry until lightly golden and cooked through (usually in about 3 minutes). Lift out *cannoli*, draining excess oil back into the pot, and very gently slide off tube form, using tongs or a paper towel. Drain on paper towels and continue until all *cannoli* are fried. (These pastries can be stored at room temperature in an airtight container; change paper towel every couple of days.)

To Make Cream Filling: In a heavy saucepan, whisk together flour, sugar, and salt until blended and smooth. Gradually stir in cold milk, whisking constantly to keep the mixture smooth. Bring mixture to a boil, still whisking, and let it boil 1 to 2 minutes. In a small bowl, whisk a little of the hot milk mixture very gradually into egg yolks. Add egg yolk mixture to the hot milk mixture and boil 1 minute. Remove from heat, and stir in butter and vanilla. Place a sheet of waxed paper or plastic wrap on the surface of the cream to prevent a skin from forming. Cool thoroughly, then chill.

Assembly: Stir cream filling gently, just until smooth. Use a teaspoon to spoon a small amount of filling into each end of *cannoli*. Press a half cherry into cream at each end, then gently press some coconut into cream. Just before serving, sprinkle generously with confectioners' sugar.   *Makes about 2½ dozen.*

FRUIT-FILLED COOKIES

This easy-to-prepare cookie is reminiscent of a fig newton — only better.

DOUGH:

¼ cup (4 tablespoons) soft butter or shortening, softened
1 cup sugar
3 eggs
1 teaspoon vanilla
3 cups flour
1½ teaspoons baking powder

FILLING:

1 box (12 ounces) pitted prunes, chopped
½ cup drained canned crushed pineapple
½ cup raisins
½ cup coarsely chopped nuts
½ (3½-ounce) jar maraschino cherries, drained and chopped
Sugar to taste
Cinnamon to taste (about 1 teaspoon)
Confectioners' sugar

To Make Dough: Place all dough ingredients in the bowl of an electric mixer. Mix slowly until blended and smooth; do not over-beat. Let dough stand a few minutes while you prepare filling. Preheat oven to 400°F.

To Make Filling: Stir together all filling ingredients in a mixing bowl (they can also be chopped and mixed in a food processor).

Assembly: Divide dough into 5 or 6 pieces. Roll out each piece in a rectangular shape about ¼-inch thick. Don't worry about any tears in the dough; they can easily be patched. Spread dough with a layer of the filling, leaving a margin of dough all around. Roll up dough, beginning with a long side, as you would a jelly roll. Pinch ends shut securely. Repeat with remaining dough and filling. Arrange rolls on buttered baking sheets, spacing them slightly apart. Bake 15 to 20 minutes or until dough has set and is very lightly colored. Cool on a rack. At serving time, dust rolls with confectioners' sugar and cut diagonally into 1-inch slices. Store airtight; these cookies also freeze well, unsliced and tightly wrapped. *Makes 4 to 5 dozen.*

CHOCOLATE ALMOND BUTTER CRUNCH

This delightful, buttery, crunchy candy has a lovely thin chocolate covering and is as good as any from a candy shop. It is a Codola family treasure.

1½ cups (about 12 ounces) chopped blanched almonds
½ pound (2 sticks) unsalted butter
1½ cups sugar
3 tablespoons light corn syrup

3 tablespoons water
1 teaspoon vanilla
4 ounces (4 squares) semisweet chocolate, coarsely chopped

Preheat oven to 350°F. Toast chopped almonds on a baking sheet until lightly golden — about 12 minutes. Set aside.

In a heavy 2-quart saucepan, combine butter, sugar, corn syrup, and water. Cook over medium heat, stirring frequently (constantly toward the end), to 300° on a candy thermometer (hard-crack stage). Remove pan from heat and stir in vanilla and 1¼ cups of the almonds. Immediately pour the mixture into a buttered 9- by 13-inch pan, spreading it evenly and quickly. Cool.

Turn the cooled mixture out onto a sheet of waxed paper. Melt chocolate in the top of a double boiler, then remove from heat. Spread chocolate over the surface of the almond crunch and sprinkle with remaining nuts. Let stand until set, then break into bite-sized pieces. Store airtight at room temperature.

Makes about 1½ pounds.

Fred Amerighi "paddling" his spaghetti sauce.

Spaghetti for 350 . . . or 10

FRED AMERIGHI
Sharon, Connecticut

The Italian feast served here is a very different one from the Christmas Eve feast offered by Mary Codola, but feast it is — and just as much a celebration.

Fred Amerighi has been putting on benefit spaghetti suppers in Sharon, Connecticut, for more than 15 years now. "The first one I did in town was for the CYO," Fred recalls, smiling as he adds, "I think they asked me pretty much just because I had an Italian name." He now masterminds seven or eight of these benefits a year; one recent supper to help with medical expenses for a six-month-old baby drew nearly 500 people and netted $4,000.

The supper Fred is going to guide us through here was held on a Saturday evening at the Sharon Center School to help the local Lions' Club raise scholarship money, and was planned to feed 350 – – that's right, three hundred and fifty! Before Fred and his crew (his daughter Linda and a ready band of Lions) were through, they had to turn a small mountain of groceries into 150 quarts of sauce, 900 meatballs, 40 pounds of edible spaghetti — all hot at once — plus all the trimmings. As you will see, despite all the chores to be done, somehow everything *did* get done — and on time.

As he readily admits, Fred didn't come to cooking for the masses as a complete neophyte: he spent a good part of World War II as a mess sergeant. Still, watching Fred Amerighi at work, one gets the feeling he has *always* known what to do when, whether it was cooking or anything else.

The main supper task is, of course, the sauce. Fred makes his the way he learned as a boy from watching his mother. It takes a gallon of ground vegetables; pounds and pounds of beef, pork, and hot and sweet sausages; plus jars on end of tomatoes in all forms; and a wide range of seasonings. It then must cook for at least 14 hours before it finally meets Fred's approval (and even then, about midway through the day of the supper, he calls in his wife to get her official "sauce okay"). Throughout the long cooking process, the sauce must be stirred laboriously, and frequently (to be sure it doesn't stick), in an 80-quart kettle. For this, Fred uses a long wooden stirring paddle especially fashioned for him by his son. "The flavor develops as you go along," Fred explains. "I try to hit a happy medium to suit all tastes."

However, the sauce, with its meatballs and sausages, is only part of the task: there is the salad to make, the bread to slice, and the beverages to ready. But, finally, at about dark on Saturday, the preparations, which began about 24 hours before, are over, and the supper — for 350 first helpings, and often seconds and thirds — is ready. Fred's dinner, as usual, is a great success. There are 350 happy stomachs, a well-fattened scholarship fund — and Fred Amerighi is still smiling.

A bit later, Fred, his apron still splattered with sauce, sat down with pencil and paper to figure out how to scale down his mammoth spaghetti sauce recipe to feed ten or so. That may have been Fred's hardest job of all; as he put it, he's "never fed so few." Thanks to Fred, those of us not about to cook spaghetti for 350 can, nonetheless, share in Fred's good fixings.

Recipes for both spaghetti suppers — the crowd pleaser and the more intimate — follow, each with its own directions.

SPAGHETTI SAUCE
WITH MEATBALLS AND SAUSAGES
(FOR 350)

The fact that the people of Sharon, Connecticut, keep coming back for more and more year after year should be proof enough that this is a topnotch spaghetti sauce.

EQUIPMENT:

An 80-quart kettle
At least 2 smaller (40-quart) kettles
A long paddle for stirring
Deep cookie sheets or sheet-cake pans for baking meatballs and sausages

A heavy-duty meat grinder and mixer
Large kettles for cooking spaghetti
Steamer for keeping spaghetti warm (optional)

INGREDIENTS:

55 pounds ground beef
25 pounds ground pork
30 pounds sweet Italian sausages
40 pounds hot Italian sausages
12 green peppers, cored and seeded
5 pounds yellow onions, skinned
2 pounds carrots, scrubbed
2 packages celery hearts
1 dozen eggs
2 boxes (15 ounces each) bread crumbs
3 cans (15 ounces each) Hunt's Tomato Sauce Special

3 jars (5/8 ounces each) Italian seasoning (Durkee's preferred)
7 to 8 teaspoons ground oregano
3 to 4 teaspoons sage
Salt and pepper as needed
1 can (46 ounces) tomato juice
1 cup olive oil
2 (No. 10) cans tomato paste
6 (No. 10) cans tomato sauce (6 pounds 3 ounces each)
8 (No. 10) cans tomato purée

Recipe continues on next page

55

½ large (1-ounce) jar
  parsley flakes
6 (No. 10) cans ground
  crushed tomatoes
10 pounds grated
  Parmesan cheese
40 pounds thin
  semolina spaghetti

Enough Italian bread,
  butter, salad, wine,
  coffee, dessert, and
  other accompani-
  ments to feed 350

METHOD (step by step, the way Fred does it):

1. Using a heavy-duty meat grinder, grind together the peppers, onions, carrots, and celery, including any leaves; transfer to a large bowl and set aside.

2. Attach a heavy blade to the mixer. Place about 15 pounds of the ground beef in the mixer bowl. Add 5 pounds of ground pork, 6 eggs, ½ (1 box) of the bread crumbs, and ½ (1½ cans) of the Hunt's Tomato Sauce Special; attach cover and beat all together. After about 2 minutes, add seasonings as follows: ⅓ jar Italian seasoning, 2 teaspoons oregano, 1 teaspoon sage, 1 teaspoon salt, and 2 teaspoons pepper. Then add in about ½ can tomato juice. Beat all together again, about 5 minutes. Shape into meatballs; makes about 450 balls 2 inches in diameter. Cover and refrigerate.

3. Following same procedure and amounts, make a second batch of about 450 meatballs. Again cover and refrigerate.

4. Pour the olive oil into the bottom of the 80-quart kettle. Add 25 pounds ground beef and 10 to 15 pounds ground pork, and using a long paddle, carefully brown the meat, breaking it up as it cooks.

5. When meat is thoroughly browned, spoon on both cans tomato paste. Add the set-aside ground vegetables with any juices, ½ (3 cans) of the plain tomato sauce, and ½ (4 cans) of the tomato purée. By now the pot is about one-third full. Spices come next: 2 jars Italian seasoning, all of the parsley, and spoonfuls of oregano, sage, and pepper. Let simmer. After 15 or so minutes, add 2 cans crushed tomatoes, rinsing out cans with a little water and adding to the sauce. After sauce has simmered about 2 hours, Fred packs up for the night, but cooking can continue as is convenient. If the sauce is left untended, the heat should be turned off and the pot covered.

6. At a convenient time, divide the sauce into more manageable thirds; add in the remaining 4 cans purée, 3 cans plain tomato sauce, and 4 cans crushed tomatoes, dividing them among the 3 kettles. Then add more of the remaining seasonings to taste and allow all to continue simmering.

7. At this point, begin to bake the prepared meatballs. Bake the trays in ovens preheated to 350°F. for about 20 minutes or until they are firm but not crusty. As each tray is done, pour off the grease and gently transfer the meatballs to large holding bowls or pans.

8. Meanwhile, cut apart the sausage links and arrange them on high-sided trays, being careful to keep the hot and sweet sausages separate. Prick each sausage with a fork so the excess grease can leak out and then load the trays into ovens, still at 350°. Let sausages bake 15 to 20 minutes, turn, and then bake another 15 to 20 minutes. When done, drain and set aside.

9. Check the sauce, adding remaining Italian seasoning and pepper as needed. Scoop about ⅓ cup Parmesan cheese into each kettle, 1 cup in all (this, Fred tells us, "to add texture and taste"). (Another batch of the cheese will be added later in the simmering; the rest is for the table shakers.) At this point, the sauce will need to be stirred every 5 or 6 minutes to be sure it doesn't stick and burn. (If the sauce should ever burn, Fred advises not to stir it; instead, carefully pour the good sauce on top into a clean pot and keep going.) Fred never covers the pots during cooking, and gradually the long simmering produces a thick sauce that doesn't separate on the plate. Continue to let sauce simmer, stirring frequently, for a total of about 14 hours.

10. Two hours or so before serving time, divide the meatballs evenly among the 3 kettles; add hot sausages to one kettle, the sweet to another, leaving one with meatballs alone so the diners can have a three-way choice. Allow all to heat through thoroughly.

11. Meanwhile, in large kettles, bring the spaghetti water to a boil. Then, just before the first guests arrive, boil spaghetti for 8 to 9 minutes, keeping it warm in a steamer as needed.

12. Serve — and enjoy!

SPAGHETTI SAUCE WITH MEATBALLS
(FOR 10)

This rich, hearty spaghetti sauce, since it specifies canned tomato products, is especially useful when fresh tomatoes are not at their best.

SAUCE:

⅓ cup olive oil
1 pound ground beef
½ pound ground pork
¼ pound ground veal
   (optional)
1 can (14 ounces)
   tomato paste
1 carrot
1 green pepper, cored
   and seeded
1 celery stalk
1 medium onion, peeled
1 can (28 ounces)
   tomato purée
1 can (28 ounces)
   tomato sauce

1 can (28 ounces)
   ground tomatoes
1 teaspoon Italian
   seasoning (Durkee's
   preferred)
Salt and pepper to taste
1 or more cloves minced
   fresh garlic to taste
   (optional)
1 teaspoon chopped
   parsley
¼ teaspoon oregano
⅛ teaspoon sage
¼ cup grated Parmesan
   cheese

MEATBALLS:

1½ pounds ground beef
½ pound ground pork
1 cup dry bread crumbs
1 egg
⅓ (15-ounce) can Hunt's
   Tomato Sauce Special,
   or more as wanted

1 teaspoon Italian
   seasoning
¼ teaspoon sage
½ teaspoon oregano
Salt and pepper to taste
Tomato juice to
   moisten, if necessary

To make sauce, heat olive oil in large kettle and add meats, stirring until browned. Add tomato paste and stir. Grind carrot, pepper, celery, and onion in a food grinder or food processor and add to sauce. Add tomato purée, tomato sauce, and ground tomatoes. Add seasonings, adjusting to taste, and simmer over low heat for 7 to 8 hours, the longer the better. After about 4 hours, stir in grated Parmesan cheese. Add meatballs several hours before serving. Do not cover kettle, and remember to stir frequently so that the sauce doesn't stick to bottom of pan.

To make meatballs, combine all ingredients in a large bowl and mix well with hands, adding tomato juice to moisten if needed. Adjust seasoning if necessary, and mix again. Shape mixture into meatballs the size of golf balls and place on a cookie sheet with 1-inch sides (or a jelly-roll pan). Bake at 350°F. for about 20 minutes, until meatballs are firm but not browned. Add to sauce as described above.

Cook enough thin spaghetti to feed the assembled company. Serve hot with sauce and additional grated Parmesan cheese. Any leftover sauce will freeze well.

VARIATION: Hot or sweet Italian sausages, pricked with a fork and browned (30 minutes or so) on cookie sheets in a 350°F. oven, may be added to the sauce along with the meatballs.

Father Kenneth Bonadies and some of his Mediterranean dishes.

Mediterranean Memories

FATHER KENNETH BONADIES
Manchester, Connecticut

In recent years many diverse ethnic cuisines have contributed their own distinctive flavors to the New England cooking pot. To add to the French-Canadian and Italian cookery we have already sampled, Father Kenneth Bonadies — fluent in six languages and an equal number of cuisines — will guide us further on along the Mediterranean where we'll enjoy several of the favorite dishes of Greece and Lebanon. What's more, since Father Bonadies earned his culinary stripes at the knees of his Lithuanian mother and Italian father, it's no surprise that our culinary travels will include a taste of their cuisines as well.

As Father Bonadies points out, there are many common denominators in Mediterranean cooking. Often very nearly the same dish is prepared but flavored differently: the Lebanese, for example, like to flavor with mint, while the Turks might use dill. Sometimes not much more than the spelling of a dish will change: the *Baba Ganouche* here will be *baba ghanoush* elsewhere, while the *Tabouli* may become *tabbouleh*.

Father Bonadies's interest in cooking has taken him far beyond his own kitchen. Each year he escorts a group of Manchester students on a field trip to Rome, where he combines tours of cathedrals and museums with a tour of some of the best Italian restaurants. He has also gathered 130 of his favorite Italian recipes into a cookbook, *Italian Culinary Secrets of the Confessional* (available through East Catholic High School, 115 New State Road, Manchester, CT 06040 for $3.50 postpaid).

"Food memories and music memories are the most intense," says Father Bonadies enthusiastically. At once an expert chef and gifted music instructor at Manchester's East Catholic High, it is obvious that this popular priest is busily helping to build both.

TUNA-CHICKEN PÂTÉ ALLE PIEDMONTE

This tasty hors d'oeuvre and sandwich spread has its origins in northern Italy. If you like you may use the Aioli made by the recipe on page 190.

2 cups cooked chicken meat	1 teaspoon salt
1 can (7 ounces) chunk white tuna	½ teaspoon white pepper
2 fillets anchovy	1 teaspoon capers
⅔ cup Aioli (or ⅔ cup mayonnaise flavored with 2 small cloves garlic, minced)	½ cup sliced pitted ripe black olives, for garnish

Put all ingredients except the capers and olives through a food grinder (set at "fine") or process to a fine "chop." *Don't purée!* Fold in the capers with a fork, and then either turn the mixture into a mold or, using a rubber spatula, shape it into a loaf. Refrigerate for 2 hours, then unmold and serve with the sliced olives for garnish. *Makes about 3 cups.*

BABA GANOUCHE

A delicious off-the-beaten-track hors d'oeuvre. However, allow ample time for any smokiness from broiling the eggplant to dissipate before your guests arrive. Also an excellent pita bread sandwich spread.

1 large eggplant	¾ teaspoon salt
1½ tablespoons sesame	2 cloves garlic, pressed,
tahini	or ¼ teaspoon garlic
3 tablespoons lemon	powder
juice	

Pierce eggplant and place it, whole, 3 to 4 inches under broiler. Broil it on all sides for a total of 30 minutes. Cool; peel skin from flesh. Put eggplant flesh into a blender with other ingredients and mix at high speed for a couple of minutes. Cool and serve with small pita bread triangles. *Makes ample hors d'oeuvre for 4.*

TABOULI

Another good change-of-pace hors d'oeuvre — and an easy one to prepare. The mint reveals its Lebanese origin.

1 cucumber, finely	2 cloves garlic, pressed,
minced	or ¼ teaspoon garlic
4 stalks celery, minced	powder
2 small tomatoes,	½ cup olive oil
minced	Juice of 2 fresh lemons
1 large bunch Italian	2 tablespoons dried or 4
parsley, finely minced	tablespoons fresh
½ cup coarse bulgur	spearmint
wheat, soaked in	4 green onions, with
about ½ cup water	stalks, minced
for 1 hour and	
squeezed dry	

Mix all ingredients in a large bowl and let sit in refrigerator 1 hour or longer before serving. *Ample hors d'oeuvre for 4.*

GAZPACHO

A pretty and pleasantly spiced cold soup. Some like to top it with a dollop of sour cream.

1 large onion
2 stalks celery
1 large green pepper (reserve and dice ¼ of the pepper)
3 cups defatted chicken stock or bouillon
1 large can (1 pound 12 ounces) whole tomatoes (reserve and dice 1 cup)
1 medium can (24 ounces) tomato juice
¼ cup olive oil
½ teaspoon cumin
¼ teaspoon Tabasco
1 cucumber (reserve ¼ and thinly slice for garnish; finely mince remaining ¾)

Cook the onion, celery, and three-fourths of the green pepper in chicken stock until soft. Then purée with the canned tomatoes (reserving 1 cup diced). Add tomato juice, oil, cumin, and Tabasco, then chill. Add the minced cucumber and diced tomatoes just before serving, and garnish each bowl with slices of cucumber.

Yield: 4 to 6 cups.

AVGOLEMONO SOUP

The lemon juice and yogurt give this Greek chicken soup a deliciously fresh taste.

3 quarts chicken stock
1 cup plain yogurt
2 eggs, beaten
¼ cup lemon juice
1 cup cooked rice

2 tablespoons finely
  minced parsley
½ cup minced cooked
  chicken meat

Bring stock to boiling. Add 2 cups of the boiling stock to the yogurt, eggs, and lemon juice, and mix well. Then combine and heat all the ingredients together in the soup pot, being careful not to boil the mixture. Serve hot. *Serves 6 to 8.*

PASTITSIO

This delightfully seasoned lamb casserole is Greek in origin and a welcome change from the more usual beef varieties — and special enough for company.

1 pound ground lamb
2 tablespoons oil
1 large clove garlic,
  minced
2 medium onions, finely
  chopped
1 teaspoon cinnamon
1 teaspoon nutmeg

1 teaspoon oregano
1 box (1 pound) ziti
1 pound feta cheese
6 eggs
½ cup grated Parmesan
  cheese
3 cups milk

Brown the ground lamb in the oil and add garlic, onions, and seasonings. Boil ziti to firm *al dente* stage. Line a deep baking dish with ziti and cover it with a layer of meat and a layer of crumbled feta. Repeat layers 3 times, leaving at least 2 inches of space in the pan. Beat together eggs, Parmesan cheese, and milk, and pour over entire contents of casserole. Bake at 375°F. for 45 minutes, setting the casserole in 1 inch of water in a large pan. *Serves 8.*

GALLINA IMPANATA "STIMPERADA"
Sicilian Chicken with Olives

This delicious Sicilian chicken dish blends the tastes of several Mediterranean cuisines.

1 chicken, cut into
  pieces
½ cup vinegar (either
  white or wine)
1 cup water
2 tablespoons dried,
  crushed mint leaves
  or ½ cup minced
  fresh mint

4 cloves garlic, minced
2 stalks celery, sliced ¼-
  inch thick
Salt and pepper to taste
½ cup pitted green
  olives

Place chicken in a large baking dish. Mix vinegar, water, mint, and garlic together with the celery and pour over the chicken. The vinegar mixture should come to only ⅓ or ½ the depth of the chicken (use a bigger pan if the liquid is too high). Add salt and pepper to taste. Bake at 400°F. for 50 to 70 minutes. Then add olives to the pan and bake 15 minutes more. *Serves 4 to 6.*

BALANDUKE
Cabbage Rolls, Lithuanian Style

The dill and smoked pig's hocks give this crowd-pleasing main dish a distinctive flavor. Be sure to start with a large roasting pan, you'll need it.

1 large, flat head
    cabbage
2 pounds hamburger (if
    meat is lean, add 2
    tablespoons vegetable
    oil)
1 cup short-grain rice,
    boiled for 5 minutes
    in 1 quart water, then
    drained
1 egg
1 cup minced onion
3 tablespoons dried dill
    weed

1 tablespoon salt
1 teaspoon white pepper
1 can (1 pound)
    sauerkraut, well
    washed
1 pound smoked Desros
    (smoked sausage —
    Kielbasa will do)
2 small smoked pig's
    hocks
1 large can (32 ounces)
    tomato juice
1 quart water

Core the cabbage and place the head in boiling water, removing the outer leaves one at a time as they become limp. Meanwhile, mix the meat and rice with the egg, onion, and 2 tablespoons of the dried dill weed; add the salt and pepper; then use to stuff the cabbage leaves.

To stuff the leaves, place 3 tablespoons of the meat mixture in the center of each leaf. Then fold in the uncovered portions of each leaf envelope-fashion: first from the bottom, then from the sides, and finally fold the top section down and over all.

Next, chop the inside of the cabbage and mix it with the sauerkraut; then line a roaster with half of the mixture. Place the cabbage rolls in the roaster with the sausage and hocks, cover with more rolls, and finally add the remaining cabbage and kraut. Sprinkle with remaining dill; pour tomato juice and water over the top and bake, covered, at 375°F. for 3 hours. Let sit, covered, for 20 minutes before serving. *Serves 8 to 10.*

FATHER B'S TUNA ROLLS

These pleasantly flavored tuna rolls make a lovely light luncheon dish. Cut in half or thirds they also make tasty hors d'oeuvres.

24 large lettuce leaves
2 cans (7 ounces each)
    tuna packed in water,
    drained
2 cups cooked rice
2 heaping tablespoons
    capers
2 shallots, chopped
½ cup minced scallions
1 tablespoon dried,
    crushed mint leaves

Salt and pepper to taste
1 cup diced celery,
    blanched and cooled
⅓ cup olive oil plus 2
    tablespoons
¼ cup lemon juice plus
    1 tablespoon
2 tablespoons chopped
    parsley, for garnish

Plunge lettuce leaves into boiling water. Remove after about 20 seconds and immediately plunge into ice water. Remove and let drain in a colander. Pat dry. Combine tuna with rice, capers, shallots, scallions, mint, salt, pepper, celery, ⅓ cup olive oil, and ¼ cup lemon juice. Using 3 tablespoons of the tuna mixture for each leaf, roll as you would for cabbage rolls (see *Balanduke* recipe), pushing in at one end with your thumb. Arrange on a serving platter and sprinkle with the remaining 2 tablespoons olive oil, 1 tablespoon lemon juice, and chopped parsley. Refrigerate for 2 hours before serving. *Makes 24 rolls.*

ZITI AND CAULIFLOWER

This unusual combination of anchovies, basil, and cauliflower has Sicilian beginnings.

1 medium onion,
  chopped
3 cloves garlic, minced
3 tablespoons olive oil
½ stick (¼ cup) butter,
  melted
2 tins (2 ounces)
  anchovies
1 small head of
  cauliflower, broken
  into small florets

3 tablespoons tomato
  paste, mixed with 2
  cups water
1 teaspoon basil
3 teaspoons capers
½ cup grated cheese
1 pound ziti, cooked

Sauté the onion and garlic in a mixture of oil and butter. Add the anchovies and cook until they are broken up. Add the cauliflower and tomato-water mixture; simmer for 40 minutes, until the sauce is blended. Finally, add the basil and capers and simmer 15 minutes more. Sprinkle the cheese over the ziti and cover with the sauce; toss and serve. *Ample for 6 to 8.*

Bashir Ahmed displays two of his Indian specialties.

A Covey of Curries

BASHIR AHMED
Northampton, Massachusetts

Another recent addition to the New England cooking pot is the fine cuisine that Bashir Ahmed brought with him to the United States in the mid-1970s from his native Kashmir, the northernmost Indian state. And a wonderfully tasty addition it is!

Indian cooking is distinguished by its use of spices, applied in subtle and imaginative combinations according to the demands of each dish and to the mood of the cook. It is important, Bashir reminds us, that the spices be gently cooked in oil to avoid having a raw or bitter taste; omitting this essential step will give an unpleasant harshness to the end result.

Bashir likes to compare the best cooking to the best weather — different every day. So it is no wonder that he rarely prepares the same dish the same way twice. However, you can come close to duplicating at least one day's menu with the following recipes. But first, look over Bashir's basic Indian spice list, which should prove helpful as you explore the subtleties of old-world Indian cookery.

THE ESSENTIAL INDIAN SPICE SHELF

Cardamom, whole pods and ground
Chilies, hot, fresh, and ground
Cinnamon, ground
Cloves, ground
Coriander (cilantro), fresh and ground
Cumin, seeds and ground
Dill
Fennel
Garlic, fresh
Ginger, ground
Ginger root, fresh
Mint, fresh and dried
Pepper, black and red
Saffron (expensive; but consider that 1 pound requires harvesting 75,000 single crocus flowers)
Turmeric
Curry powder: in India, a personalized blend of spices called a *masala,* adjusted to individual tastes and to suit whatever dish is being made. If you buy prepared curry powder, be sure it is fresh. (Bashir Ahmed recommends Sun brand Madras curry powder.)

Most large cities have Indian and food-specialty shops that carry these hard-to-find ingredients — both fresh and dried.

LAMB WITH TOMATOES

An excellent lamb curry (in Indian cooking "curry" means a highly seasoned stew, not a particular flavor). The blend of spices is commanding but with no particular spice dominating. Serve accompanied with the Radish Chutney (following), rice, and a refreshing raita (one follows).

2 to 3 pounds boned lamb
Olive oil as needed (about ⅓ cup)
4 onions, peeled and chopped
Salt to taste
4 to 5 large ripe tomatoes, peeled and cut into chunks
2 to 3 garlic cloves, chopped
1 tablespoon Madras curry powder
1 tablespoon chopped fresh ginger root (about 1-inch piece of peeled root)

¼ teaspoon cloves
1 teaspoon fennel
1 teaspoon black pepper
1 teaspoon cinnamon
Seeds from 4 large black cardamom pods (crush pods to remove seeds; discard pods)
1 teaspoon ground cumin
1 teaspoon ground coriander seed
1 tablespoon dried mint
1 handful chopped fresh coriander (cilantro or Chinese parsley)

Trim fat from lamb; cut into chunks. Heat about ¼ inch olive oil in a large heavy kettle and add lamb pieces, stirring to brown well. Remove lamb chunks to a large bowl and add onions to remaining olive oil in kettle. Salt well. When onions are soft and golden, remove from oil with a slotted spoon and add to lamb. Stew tomatoes and garlic in remaining oil, adding a little more oil if needed. Add curry powder, fresh ginger root, cloves, fennel, black pepper, cinnamon, cardamom seeds, ground cumin, ground coriander, and mint, and stir well. Return lamb and onions to kettle and mix well. Cover and let simmer until lamb and spices are well cooked. Then, add fresh coriander. *Serves 6 to 8.*

RADISH CHUTNEY

This chutney is delicious with many Indian dishes, but it is especially good with lamb. But be forewarned: it's very hot. And be sure to remove the hot pepper seeds or it'll be hotter still.

6 to 8 red radishes, trimmed	Several hot peppers, sliced (remove seeds
1 large white radish (Daikon or Chinese), peeled and cut up	first) Handful fresh mint, plus extra for garnish
Handful walnuts	½ teaspoon salt

Place all ingredients in a food processor and process until finely ground. (If peppers are very hot, handle them carefully to avoid burning your eyes and skin with the volatile oils.) Mound chutney in bowl and garnish with a few fresh mint leaves. Serve as a condiment. *Makes 1 to 1½ cups.*

VEGETABLE CURRY

This vegetable curry makes a welcome addition to a many-curry meal but also makes an excellent centerpiece for a simpler luncheon or supper. For a larger yield, allow one cup vegetables per person and increase the other ingredients proportionately.

4 cups (approximately) assorted fresh raw vegetables: broccoli, cauliflower, brussels sprouts, carrots, sweet red peppers, and others as desired	6 cloves garlic, chopped ¼ cup olive oil, or more if needed 1 tablespoon Madras curry powder 2 teaspoons red pepper

Wash and peel vegetables as necessary. Separate broccoli and cauliflower into florets, slice carrots, and slice peppers. Place mixed vegetables in a large pot and add garlic and oil, using enough oil so vegetables won't burn onto the bottom of the pan. Add curry powder and red pepper and mix well. Cover pot tightly and steam vegetables over low heat until tender. *Serves 4.*

PALAK PANIR
Spinach and Tofu

Another wonderful Indian curry — this time with spinach and tofu.

Corn oil or olive oil, as
needed (about ¾ cup)
16 ounces tofu, sliced
½-inch thick and cut
in 1-inch squares
2½ pounds fresh
spinach, washed and
picked over
4 cloves garlic, chopped
2 teaspoons Madras
curry powder
1 teaspoon ground
ginger

½ teaspoon fennel
½ teaspoon ground
coriander
1 teaspoon red pepper
½ teaspoon black
pepper
Scant ½ teaspoon cumin
seeds
½ teaspoon ground
cardamom
½ teaspoon salt

In a large skillet, heat ½ inch of oil until hot. Add tofu slices and cook, covered, turning occasionally. Meanwhile, steam the spinach in a large covered kettle. When tofu is cooked, remove pieces from oil with a slotted spoon; reserve leftover oil. In the skillet, add garlic to steamed spinach. Then add curry powder, ginger, fennel, coriander, peppers, cumin, cardamom, and salt. Add tofu and mix well. Drizzle on leftover oil and keep mixture warm over low heat. This dish may also be served at room temperature. *Serves 8.*

BASHA'S RICE

This tasty rice bears the same name as Bashir's Basha's Exquisite Gifts shop in Northampton, and it's almost as full of pleasant surprises. But be sure to use the natural pistachios — not the pink — or you won't get the lovely warm saffron color.

2 cups white rice,
 washed and picked
 over as necessary
1 generous handful each
 shelled plain
 pistachio nuts, whole
 almonds, and cashews
3 cups water
 (approximately)

1 handful raisins
3 tablespoons butter
3 generous pinches
 saffron
1 handful fresh
 chopped coriander
 (cilantro)

Wash rice in hot water to clean and soften (most Indian rice is merely husked and needs to be cleaned). Put nuts in water and bring to a boil; simmer briefly. Add raisins, butter, and saffron. Add rice by handfuls. Lower heat and cook, covered, until rice is tender. Add chopped coriander and stir. Serve hot. *Serves 10 to 12.*

RAITA
Cucumber-Yogurt Salad

A curry meal almost begs for the contrast of a cool, refreshing dish. This raita serves that need nicely. Indian raitas are made of various main ingredients, bananas among them, but cucumber is by far the most frequently used.

2 large cucumbers, peeled or unpeeled
1 pint plain yogurt
Scant teaspoon ground cumin
Scant teaspoon ground coriander
Scant teaspoon black pepper
½ teaspoon cumin seed
½ teaspoon salt
Scant teaspoon red pepper (used primarily for color; substitute thinly sliced fresh hot red peppers or finely chopped tomato if desired)
Fresh coriander (cilantro), for garnish

Early in the day, grate cucumbers and stir in yogurt, ground cumin, ground coriander, black pepper, cumin seed, salt, and red pepper. Mix well; let marinate in refrigerator for several hours. Garnish with chopped fresh coriander before serving. *Serves 4 to 6.*

Samuel Thacher, his beloved Cape Cod shoreline close at hand.

Quahaugs and Cape Cod Cod

SAMUEL THACHER
Yarmouthport, Massachusetts

Just as the varied ethnic cuisines we've met so far have added to the rich fabric of New England cookery, so too have the culinary traditions of those who "must go down to the sea." Many so driven have been lured to the multitude of weathered harbor-home villages dotting the long, accessible New England coast. Yarmouthport is just such a village, and it is here that Sam Thacher, an eighth-generation Cape Codder now in his eighties, lives on a street where, over the years, 50 different Atlantic sea captains have made their homes.

It's no wonder that when Sam prepares his famous Cape Cod dinners things of the sea head the menu. For Sam, perhaps his clam dishes hold the most fascination; for, whenever possible, he makes them from the big sea clams that live on the farthest flats of Cape Cod Bay. These are the clams exposed for diggers only two or three choice full-moon nights each month, and only at the end of a two-mile or more walk — a walk much longer on the return when the buckets are heavy with clams. Until very recent days, Sam harvested his own; now he leaves the harvesting to friends and guests, and contents himself with their preparation.

But Sam Thacher is no jack-of-one-trade cook. His cookies have, for many years, filled boxes-from-home for various of the family grandchildren, and he continues to make the desserts he used to make even when his wife was doing the rest of the cooking. Perhaps Sam's most famous sweetmeat is his Gramp's Apple Pie — a pie on which there is a standing $7.00 "bounty" (offered by a

Yarmouthport merchant) for as many as Sam will make. Sam has never claimed the "bounty," preferring to make his pies as friendship tokens. You may do the same with the recipe he shares here, along with the rest.

SCALLOPED OYSTERS

Like their brothers of Lewis Carroll "Walrus and Carpenter" fame, these oysters will be "eaten every one."

½ cup bread crumbs	Salt and pepper to taste
1 cup Ritz cracker crumbs	4 tablespoons oyster liquor
½ cup butter, melted	2 tablespoons milk or cream
1 pint oysters, drained	

Mix bread and cracker crumbs together, and stir in melted butter. Put about a third of this mixture in a thin layer in the bottom of a medium-sized shallow buttered baking dish. Cover with half of the oysters and sprinkle with salt and pepper. Add half each of the oyster liquor and milk or cream. Repeat layers; cover top with remaining crumbs. (Never allow more than 2 layers of oysters for scalloped oysters. If 3 layers are used, the middle layer will be underdone when the others are properly cooked.) Bake for 25 to 30 minutes at 350°F. *Serves 6.*

CLAM PIE

When they are available, Sam uses his favorite sea clams for this pie. These clams grow to be five to six inches wide and up to a pound or more — hard work to harvest, but Sam thinks, well worth it.

Pastry for a double-
  crust pie (see Sam's
  Pie Crust below)
2 cups ground clams
  (sea clams preferred)
¼ cup clam liquor
1 tablespoon butter,
  melted

1 egg, well beaten
½ cup (heaping) Ritz
  cracker crumbs
1 cup milk
Salt and pepper to taste

Place bottom crust in a 9-inch pie plate. Combine remaining ingredients and season to taste; pour into the pie crust. Following directions for Sam's Pie Crust, cover with top crust, seal well, and vent with fork tines. Bake in a 350°F. oven for about 1 hour.

Serves 8.

VARIATION: For Scalloped Clams, omit pie crusts. Place filling in a 1½-quart greased baking dish and dot with butter. Bake at 350°F. for 20 to 25 minutes.

SAM'S PIE CRUST

A good, basic pie dough.

2 cups flour, plus extra
  for dredging crust
¾ teaspoon salt
⅔ cup lard

5 to 6 tablespoons milk,
  plus extra to sprinkle
  pie crust
2 teaspoons Crisco
1 teaspoon butter

Combine flour, salt, and lard until crumbly. Add milk and form into a ball. Chill mixture; then divide in half and roll out to make 2 crusts. When the pie is filled and sealed, spread mixture of Crisco and butter on the top crust. Dredge with flour and then sprinkle with milk or water. The topping makes the crust flaky and helps it brown.   *Makes enough dough for 1 double-crust 9-inch pie.*

HOGSBACK SON OF A SEA COOK
Salt Codfish with Pork Scraps

The tomatoes add nice color to this pleasing fish casserole.

1 pound salt codfish	1½ cups canned
1 onion, sliced	tomatoes
2 to 3 tablespoons	3 slices raw salt pork,
butter, melted	chopped
3 medium potatoes,	¼ cup bread crumbs
boiled	Pepper to taste

Soak codfish in cold water overnight. Place fish in pan and cover with water. Heat slowly but do not boil. Pour off water and repeat process until fish is no longer salty to the taste. Drain and cut into small pieces. Sauté the onion for a few minutes in 1 tablespoon of the melted butter without browning it. Add the onion to the fish, tossing them together lightly. Butter a 2-quart baking dish and arrange layers of fish, then slices of potatoes, some of the tomatoes, and some of the pork. Continue layering until dish is filled. Use 1 to 2 tablespoons of the remaining melted butter to moisten bread crumbs lightly; then sprinkle casserole top with buttered crumbs and pepper. Bake in a moderate (350°F.) oven until browned.

Serves 4 to 6.

HARWICHPORT POTATOES

Russet potatoes work nicely for this delicately flavored fix-ahead potato dish. The pimientos add a good dash of color; the potatoes cook up tender but not mushy.

4 cups raw potatoes, cubed (½- to ¾-inch pieces)	½ pound cream cheese, diced
1 onion, chopped	2 cups thin white sauce
2 pimientos, cut into thin strips	

Cook the potatoes and onion in salted water for 5 minutes. Drain. Pour into a buttered 2-quart casserole dish. Add pimientos. Add the cream cheese to the white sauce and pour over the potatoes. Bake in a moderate (350°F.) oven for 45 minutes.   *Serves 6 to 8.*

SAM'S HARVARD BEETS

This recipe is very similar to Emma Tourangeau's, except that it has no cloves.

12 small beets, cooked and cut in slices or cubes	¼ cup vinegar
	¼ cup water
	2 tablespoons butter
¼ to ⅓ cup sugar	
½ tablespoon cornstarch	

Mix sugar and cornstarch together in a medium-sized saucepan. Add vinegar and water, and boil 5 minutes. Add beets to hot sauce and let stand 30 minutes. Just before serving, bring to a boil and add butter.   *Serves 3 to 4.*

BROWN BREAD

*Although it is not steamed and has no raisins, this is the brown bread
Sam Thacher's mother served with the family's Saturday night beans.*

2 teaspoons baking soda	3 cups sour milk
1½ cups white flour	2 teaspoons salt
1 cup brown sugar	3½ to 4 cups graham
2 eggs	flour
½ cup molasses	

Sift baking soda with white flour. Combine with remaining ingredients. Form into 2 large loaves. Bake in greased loaf pans at
350°F. for 1 hour or until done.   *Yield: 2 loaves.*

RHUBARB PIE

This is a refreshing summer pie with or without the strawberries.

Make dough for a double-crust 9-inch pie. Then, in a large bowl,
combine 4 cups of rhubarb (cut into 1-inch pieces), 3 tablespoons
flour, and 1 heaping cup sugar. (If you like, use 1 cup hulled and
sliced strawberries in place of 1 cup rhubarb.) Add 2 well-beaten
eggs. Stir well to mix thoroughly. Let set for about 10 minutes.
Line pie plate with pastry and pour in the rhubarb mixture. Cover
with a top crust and vent. Seal crusts well. Bake at 350° to 375°F.
for 30 to 40 minutes or until done.   *Serves 6.*

GRAMP'S APPLE PIE

This is a delicious apple pie, but very hearty and rich.

Use a deep pie plate and McIntosh apples. Peel, core, and thinly slice 5 to 6 apples. Prepare dough for a 9-inch double-crust pie (use Sam's Pie Crust above or your own favorite). Fit the bottom crust into the pan. Mix 1 cup white sugar with 1 tablespoon flour and spread 3 tablespoons of this mixture on the bottom crust. Fill the plate half full of apple slices, and on them spread half the remaining sugar and flour mixture. Now scatter 10 pieces of cheddar cheese (pieces the size of red kidney beans) over the apple slices. Fill the plate with the remaining apple slices until nicely rounded and spread the balance of the sugar and flour plumb in the center of the pie. Drizzle on 1 tablespoon of molasses, then scatter 10 small pieces of butter on top. Mix ¼ teaspoon cinnamon and ¼ teaspoon nutmeg with 1 teaspoon sugar. Sprinkle this over all. Put on the top crust and vent (with fork pricks) to let the steam escape. Mix 1 teaspoon butter with 2 teaspoons Crisco and spread onto the pie crust. Dust with flour and sprinkle with water. Bake at 350°F. until done (about 45 minutes).   *Serves 6 to 8.*

Lena Novello offering two of her renowned fish dishes.

The Best Fish Around

LENA NOVELLO
Gloucester, Massachusetts

About 75 miles north of Sam Thacher's Yarmouthport, across Cape Cod Bay and then on across Massachusetts Bay, lies the historic New England fishing port of Gloucester, Massachusetts. And in Gloucester, everyone knows who cooks the best fish around — Lena Novello.

Lena's interest in fish is not only culinary. She is part of a long fishing heritage, "with boats on both sides of the family." Her father joined the Gloucester fishing fleet in the 20s, and her husband is a fishing-boat skipper.

In the early days, life for Lena on the fringe of the fleet was one chiefly of fear: it is a dangerous way to make a living and was even more so a few years back. In more recent days, Lena and many of the other fishermen's wives have taken a more active role, grouping together into the Gloucester Fishermen's Wives Association. Under its banner, they have lobbied for federal funds to help improve the antiquated fishing boats, for a 200-mile fishing limit, and — more generally — have worked to promote the appreciation of fish as an inexpensive, nutritious, and delicious foodstuff.

What better way for accomplished fish cooks to achieve their aims than through a series of blockbuster fish fries? Under Lena's direction, these fries have been so successful that Lena is now sought out all across the Cape Ann area to stage benefit fish fries for a long list of local charities. What's more, she and other association members were persuaded to produce *The Taste of Gloucester*, a cookbook containing many of their best fish recipes and incorporating various suggestions on the proper purchase, care, and preparation of fish. Lena's personal list of do's and don'ts for handling fish follows, as does a sampling of recipes from *The Taste of Gloucester* (copies of the 84-page book are available by sending $5.65 to P.O. Box 1181, Gloucester, MA 01930; 25¢ extra for Massachusetts residents).

LENA'S DO'S AND DON'TS
FOR HANDLING FISH

1. Whenever possible, buy fish with the bone in: it's better tasting. "The bone," according to Lena, "gives a certain flavor," and "the flesh" she continues, "shrinks away from the skeleton in the cooking process, making it simpler to bone the fish before serving."

2. If a particular recipe requires fillets, Lena suggests starting with a whole fish. After filleting the fish, the remains of the cleaned fish can be boiled in water (to cover) with a little salt, pepper, onion, and celery. This provides a hearty stock — a good base for chowder — and can be frozen for future use.

3. When buying fish, plan on a third of a pound per person for fillets ("Fish doesn't shrink, so when you start with a pound, you end with a pound"). When buying fish whole, allow at least half a pound per person.

---

4. To check a fish for freshness, Lena says the secret is in the eyes: they should be clear, bright, and bulging. Also check around the gills — the redder the better. Yellow indicates a tired fish: don't buy it. Doubtful home-caught fish can be tested in a bucket of water; if fresh, the fish will sink.

5. Never store fish from the market in its plastic container. Drain fish immediately and pat it dry with a paper towel to absorb the moisture (excess moisture is what causes fish to spoil). Carefully dried fish will keep in the refrigerator for 3 or 4 days. Lena places fillets in a paper towel-lined colander and then covers all loosely with a dish towel.

6. One way that Lena holds fresh fish, or leftover uncooked fish, even longer is to dip it in seasoned flour and fry it. It can then be stored for future use in plastic bags in the freezer.

7. To serve fish on a busy day, Lena prepares the dish she wants to serve ahead, then wraps individual portions in foil. When ready to serve, she places the pieces in a pan with a little water and heats them in a 375°F. oven for about 10 minutes.

8. To be sure their fish-loving family has ample fish on hand year round, Lena prepares great batches of salt cod each fall. (Adventurous fish lovers may do the same with Captain Novello's Recipe for Salting Cod, which follows further on in this segment.)

JUBILEE GUMBO

When Lena makes her Jubilee Gumbo she no longer follows a recipe; she simply tosses together whatever comes to mind by instinct. The recipe here is only a guideline: Lena urges all to try their own combinations — the greater the variety, the better.

1 pound ocean fish fillets (for example, haddock, snapper, cod, and/or sole)
½ pound small peeled shrimp and 1 pound shucked clams or other assorted seafoods
1 can (1 pound) tomatoes
1 medium green pepper, chopped
1 medium onion, peeled and chopped
¼ cup olive oil, more or less
2 cups water and white wine, half and half, to cover
¼ teaspoon salt, or to taste
½ teaspoon hot pepper sauce

Make your Jubilee "catch" at the market, making sure the fish and seafood are fresh. Combine canned tomatoes with green pepper, onion, and olive oil in a deep saucepan or soup kettle, and place over low heat. Simmer until tender, about 15 minutes. Add fish and seafood; then add water and white wine just to cover. Season with salt and hot pepper sauce. Cover and cook approximately another 30 minutes. Serve in soup plates over a mound of fluffy rice.   *Serves 6 to 8.*

BAKED FISH FIESTA

Like Lena's other fish recipes, this one is designed to be attractive and aromatic, as well as delicious.

2 pounds cusk, cod, or
   other firm fish fillets,
   fresh or frozen
¾ cup fine dry bread
   crumbs
¼ cup (4 tablespoons)
   grated Parmesan
   cheese
2 tablespoons chopped
   parsley
1 teaspoon salt

¼ teaspoon pepper
1 small clove garlic,
   minced
¼ cup cooking oil
3 slices bacon, diced
1 can (8 ounces) stewed
   tomatoes or 1 cup
   chopped tomatoes
2 hard-boiled eggs,
   sliced

Cut fish into 6 equal portions (if frozen, thaw first). Combine bread crumbs, 2 tablespoons cheese, parsley, salt, pepper, and garlic. Dip fish in oil, drain, and dip in crumb mixture. Place fillets in individual baking pans or on a baking sheet. Fry bacon pieces until half-done; drain well. Top each fish portion with an equal amount of bacon, tomato pieces, and egg slices. Sprinkle with remaining 2 tablespoons of cheese. Bake in moderate (375°F.) oven for 20 minutes or until fish flakes easily when tested with a fork. *Serves 6.*

SPINACH-FISH CASSEROLE

This casserole makes an excellent one-dish fish meal — and the spinach adds nice color.

1 to 2 pounds hake fillets	1 package (1 pound) fresh spinach
1 medium onion, chopped fine	2 medium potatoes, cooked and mashed
½ cup finely chopped celery	1 beaten egg
Salt and pepper to taste	½ pound grated cheddar cheese
¼ cup olive oil	

In a large skillet, sauté fish, onion, celery, salt, and pepper in oil for about 10 minutes. Set aside to cool slightly. Cook spinach and drain, then squeeze out all water. Set aside to cool. Mix mashed potatoes, sautéed fish, and beaten egg together. In a buttered casserole dish, place a layer of the fish mixture, then a layer of spinach. Sprinkle with half the grated cheese. Cover with the rest of fish mixture, then the spinach, and sprinkle the remaining cheese over top. Bake at 350°F. for 25 to 30 minutes until just heated and the cheese melts. Serve with a white or fish sauce.	*Serves 4.*

FILLETS OF COD CAPE ANN–STYLE

An especially nice fish dish for the uninitiated. The sauce is an impressively rich but easy one.

1 pound cod	2 tablespoons white wine
6 mushrooms, chopped	2 tablespoons flour
1 to 2 tablespoons chopped parsley	½ cup milk
2 tablespoons finely chopped shallot	Lemon slices, cucumber balls, and tomato wedges, for garnish
Salt and pepper to taste	

Arrange fillets of cod in a small buttered baking dish. Sprinkle with mushrooms, parsley, shallot, salt, and pepper. Moisten with white wine. Bake at 350°F. for 15 minutes or until fish flakes when tested with a fork; remove fish to serving platter. Combine flour and milk with the remaining juices in the baking pan. Cook, stirring, until the sauce is smooth and slightly thickened. Pour sauce over fish and garnish with lemon slices, cucumber balls, and tomato wedges. *Serves 2 to 3.*

SWEET-SOUR FISH

This flavorful Chinese-style dish with its rich mahogany sauce can be prepared in a wok if you prefer. Be careful not to add too much salt in the sauce; some soy sauces and sherries are saltier than others.

2 pounds haddock or other firm-fleshed fish fillets

2 tablespoons cornstarch

2 tablespoons peanut oil

1 scallion or ½ medium onion, chopped

3 cloves garlic, crushed

1 slice ginger, cut in thin strips

MIX FOR SAUCE:

3 tablespoons soy sauce

2 tablespoons sherry

½ cup brown sugar

4 tablespoons vinegar

2 tablespoons cornstarch

1 cup chicken stock

1 teaspoon salt, or less to taste (optional)

Cut fillets into 2-inch and 3-inch pieces. Coat with cornstarch. Heat a large skillet (or wok, if you prefer) to 350°F. Add oil, heat thoroughly. Fry fish on both sides until golden brown. While the fish is cooking, combine the sauce ingredients in a small bowl. Set aside. Remove the fish from the pan and quick-fry scallion, garlic, and ginger until golden brown. Add the sweet-sour sauce and bring to a boil. Stir constantly until thick. Reduce the heat to low. Add the fish gently into the sauce and simmer for 1 minute. Serve hot. *Serves 4 to 6.*

CAPTAIN NOVELLO'S RECIPE
FOR SALTING COD

TO SALT:

1. Butterfly the cod (cut in half lengthwise, leaving bone on one half and skin and tail attached). Cut off head and eviscerate.

2. Cover bottom of a leakproof plastic tub with coarse salt. Stack the pieces of fish; salt each layer heavily.

3. The juice from the fish and the salt will combine to form a brine. If the fish float, put weight on top to force them down into the brine.

4. Soak fish in brine, uncovered, in cellar or other cool place for 3 days.

5. Take fish out of brine and let it sit uncovered for 24 hours.

6. Scrub fish, using a brush. Skin will be whitish; scrub until the natural color returns. Meat will be slimy; scrub *gently* until all slime is removed.

7. Thread a metal hook or strong line through the tail of each piece and hang the fish from a clothesline. This must be done on a dry, cool day, when a northwest wind is blowing, if possible.

8. Let the fish hang for 10 to 12 days, depending on the thickness of the pieces. Bring fish indoors if rain is expected; it will spoil if it gets wet.

9. After the hanging period is over, skin the fish. Cut into pieces and pack in plastic bags. The Novellos store their fish in the freezer to avoid having it turn a rusty, brownish color.

TO RECONSTITUTE:

Soak the amount of fish wanted for 2 days, changing the water at least 3 times a day to get the excess salt out.

SERVING SUGGESTIONS:
Flour and fry. Boil, strain, and serve with olive oil, lemon juice, peppers, and olives. Cook in tomato sauce. (Cook fish 15 to 20 minutes, less for thin pieces.) *Do not* use salt in recipes when cooking with reconstituted salt cod.

SAVORY FISH SALAD

A refreshing and attractive luncheon dish. Especially good served with tomato and cucumber slices, and fresh hot biscuits.

1½ pounds Boston bluefish (pollock) or other fish fillets, fresh or frozen
3 hard-boiled eggs, chopped
2 tablespoons sweet pickle relish, drained
⅛ teaspoon pepper
¾ cup mayonnaise

3 cups diced celery
¼ cup diced green pepper
¾ cup cooked peas
¼ teaspoon salt
1 tablespoon lemon juice
Several dashes liquid hot pepper sauce (optional)

MARINADE:
1 cup seasoned French dressing
¼ cup lemon juice or vinegar

2 tablespoons salad oil
1 teaspoon soy sauce
1 teaspoon dill weed

Thaw fish if frozen. Poach fillets until fork-tender in water to cover. Drain. Combine marinade ingredients and pour over hot fillets. Let stand several hours or until cold, turning fillets several times during standing period. Cube cold fillets. Add remaining ingredients and toss to mix. Serve in lettuce cups, or on shredded lettuce with extra dressing and a slice of lemon. *Serves 4 to 6.*

Bertha Nunan waiting for the lobsters to come in.

Perfect Lobster Every Time

BERTHA NUNAN
Cape Porpoise, Maine

Since 1974, when her husband died, Bertha Nunan — with the help of her son Richard and others — has been running Nunan's Lobster Hut on Cape Porpoise's Route 9. The Hut, begun in 1953 by Bertha's father-in-law, Captain George Nunan, is a modest, weather-beaten building sandwiched between the road and a reedy salt marsh. It is open each summer from Memorial Day weekend through September, and in 1978, was one of only three New England restaurants awarded a four-star rating by Jane and Michael Stern in *Roadfood*, their guide to the "best down-home cooking in America."

If you're seeking a fancy decor or a long list of entrées, you'll not find it at Nunan's Hut: the tables are hard, wooden booths; the trimmings are simple — a bag of potato chips and a hard roll and butter about does it; the desserts — pies and brownies — are baked by Bertha at home each morning; and the lobsters — many caught by Richard from traps in the icy waters offshore — are there for all to see in the lobster tank in the Hut's small, steamy kitchen. But if it's good food you're after, this is the place to come.

Each summer, Bertha gets almost as many requests for her secrets to boiling the perfect lobster as she does for the lobsters themselves. They are secrets she's happy to share. She offers them below, along with pointers on how best to eat the lobster once it is boiled, another query she frequently hears.

For those unable to pay a personal visit to Bertha Nunan's Lobster Hut, her how-to steps can be used to enjoy a perfect lobster at home. And, although they aren't served at The Hut, Bertha also makes a lobster stew and a baked stuffed lobster worth trying; those recipes follow here as well.

BERTHA'S STEPS TO THE PERFECT LOBSTER

1. When buying lobster, remember that from winter to summer lobsters are hard-shelled. They are firmly packed with meat during that time, so fewer lobsters are needed to make a pound of meat. (However, Bertha prefers them when they are soft-shelled, because "they're sweeter then.")

2. When boiling lobsters, the trick is not to murder them brutally. "They should," Bertha says, "be given a nice, slow way out."

3. Lobsters should never be drowned in too much water. Boiling them in a lot of water "boils the flavor out" and "waterlogs them."

4. Fill lobster pot with about 2 inches of water (Bertha uses 2 inches whether she's cooking 2 lobsters or 14).

5. Add salt. Bertha takes the saltcellar and pours it 3 times around the pot; then at the end she pours in about another 3 teaspoonfuls.

6. When water is boiling, add the lobster. Cover and steam lobster for 20 minutes ("not a minute less or a minute more," Bertha adds emphatically).

7. When lobsters are done, draw up the melted butter and serve with butter and vinegar.

8. Wash the pot after every steaming. Bertha is convinced this is the difference between The Hut's lobsters and those at many other restaurants. "Lobsters are

scavengers," she reminds us, "and leave a lot of sediment in the pot." She is firm: "Use fresh salted water for every batch."

9. One final rule: never precook and then reheat lobster. To save time, Bertha explains, some people precook their lobsters and then warm them up for a minute or two when their company arrives. "That's the worst thing one can do," Bertha emphasizes. "The lobster just fills with water. If you're eating in a restaurant," she elaborates, "and, when you crack open your lobster, water spurts out everywhere, you can bet that's what they did."

BERTHA'S POINTERS
ON HOW BEST TO EAT LOBSTER

1. To remove the lobster meat from the tail section, break off the tail with the back up ("It's less messy"), break off the flippers at the end of the tail, and then slide the meat out whole.

2. To get the meat out of the claws ("perhaps the easiest"), crack the claws with a nutcracker and pull out the meat. (Bertha cracks them for her customers before sending the orders out of the kitchen.)

3. To get the meat out of the knuckles ("the sweetest meat of all"), snap them and remove the meat with a pick.

4. To obtain the meat from the walking legs, break off the legs and suck out the meat.

5. To retrieve the greenish liver, called tomalley and thought a delicacy, break the body apart and scoop it out.

LOBSTER STEW

Although Bertha doesn't like it for anything else, frozen lobster can be used for this stew if necessary. But remember, Bertha warns, frozen lobster can be kept only about a month before it gets rubbery.

¼ pound butter (not margarine)
1 pound freshly picked lobster meat

1½ quarts milk

Melt the butter in a large skillet. Let lobster meat simmer in the butter, cooking the lobster slowly. The meat should get very juicy, and there should be no butter left in the pan. As the lobster meat absorbs the butter, heat the milk slowly, but do not let it boil. When the lobster meat is cooked, it should be beet red. Add the lobster to the milk. If you make it correctly, you won't need any seasoning, or paprika for color. The stew will taste even better if stored in the refrigerator overnight and then reheated.

Makes 4 large servings.

BAKED STUFFED LOBSTER

Bertha uses the tomalley, *or liver, of the lobster (what people call "the green stuff") to help make her stuffing. Lobster pounds usually have tomalley available, but that in the lobsters should be ample.*

4 lobsters, 1¼ to 1½
    pounds apiece
1 cup tomalley, or what
    is available from the 4
    lobsters
½ pound unsalted
    butter, melted
1 stick (½ cup)
    margarine, melted

3 stacks salt-free saltine
    crackers (¾ of a 1-
    pound box)
1 to 2 teaspoons
    Worcestershire sauce,
    or more to taste
1 tablespoon cooking
    sherry
1 tablespoon
    mayonnaise

Cook the lobsters. Split down the middle and remove the intestinal tract and the "lady," the small sac near the head. For the filling, mix the tomalley, melted shortenings, and the crackers, well crumbled. Add the Worcestershire sauce, cooking sherry, and mayonnaise. Mix well. Fill the split lobsters with the stuffing mixture, padding it up over the top. Wrap the claws in foil so that they won't dry out, and bake at 400°F. until stuffing is crisp on top (about 20 minutes or so).   *Serves 4.*

Alex Delicata preparing pasta.

Camp Cookery with Class

ALEX DELICATA
Freeport, Maine

An avid fisherman and hunter, Alex Delicata seems the ideal New England cook to intersect the fish and seafood aficionados who immediately precede him in this collection and the Rhode Island wild game bird expert who follows. He combines the best of both, with the difference that he often practices his art out in the wild rather than in the security of a well-stocked kitchen. But whether in the field or back at home, Alex applies the same high standards to fish and game cookery that he applies to all of his culinary endeavors.

Alex and his wife, Irene, arrived at the Maine woods and waterways by a circuitous route, first living in Massachusetts, then in New York City, and finally, in 1965, moving on to Maine. Always interested in good, adventurous cooking, they weren't long in Maine before they began serving game dinners to their new friends and neighbors. Happily, Alex found that his favorite flavoring trio — garlic, parsley, and basil — performed just as effectively in his new milieu, and that his star secret ingredient — horseradish — worked well, too.

Now, after years of practice, Alex has developed a few basic rules for handling the various New England wild provender he cooks: (1) he eats whatever he catches (or kills) and tries to use the *whole* fish or animal; (2) he handles game the way he would any fine cut of meat, from beginning to end (this means not dragging a deer around in the woods all day and expecting it to stay tender); (3) he tries never to overcook fish or game (except for bear, which is susceptible to trichinosis and should be cooked to 150°F.); and (4) he goes easy on fancy sauces and broils fish and meat (game and otherwise) whenever possible, to let the flavor come through.

Alex Delicata shares these pointers, and much more, with crowds sometimes numbering as many as 400, at a series of camp cookery clinics he runs for L. L. Bean, the popular hunting and fishing outfitters of Freeport, Maine. Recently, much of Alex's know-how and many of his fine recipes have found their way into the *L.L. Bean Game and Fish Cookbook*, easily ordered by writing L. L. Bean, Freeport, ME 04033. However, you can enjoy a good sampling by trying some of the recipes given here.

TROUT AND FIDDLEHEADS

Alex considers brook trout the best fish you can eat. The fiddleheads (similar in taste to asparagus) are superb when picked fresh (canned are available from L. L. Bean, Freeport, ME 04033).

4 to 6 fresh 10-inch trout	¼ teaspoon rosemary
¼ cup white flour	½ cup salad oil
¼ cup corn flour	1 bunch (20 to 30) fiddleheads
¼ teaspoon salt	4 quarts boiling water
¼ teaspoon pepper	Butter
¼ teaspoon garlic powder	

Clean fish well in cold water. Mix the flours and spices thoroughly. Dredge the fish in the flour mix (or shake in paper bag with spices and flour). Fry trout in hot oil, turning once when skin begins to crisp.

Drop fiddleheads into boiling water. Boil for 3 minutes only. Remove from water and drain. Fiddleheads will be crunchy but cooked. (Canned fiddleheads need not be cooked, only heated.) Dot with pats of butter. *Serves 4 to 6.*

SALMON PÂTÉ

Make a batch of this whenever you have the remains of a whole salmon to play with. Then throw a party; it'll be a hit.

Place the backbone and any scraps of flesh from a whole salmon in a saucepan with water to cover. Bring to a boil and cook for a couple of minutes, until the flesh is opaque. Drain; remove cooked flesh from bones and let cool. Mash cooked fish with a fork and moisten with a little mayonnaise, about ½ teaspoon horseradish for each ½ cup fish, and chopped parsley. Serve with crackers.

Yield varies with amount of salmon used.

BROILED SALMON FILLETS

Alex usually slices salmon into fillets rather than crosswise into steaks. Be sure to save any extra pieces for the lovely pâté just preceding.

2 large salmon fillets (not steaks)	Fresh chopped parsley or parsley flakes
Garlic powder	Juice of 1 lemon
Basil (fresh, if available)	Butter

If using a whole salmon, fillet the fish, cutting out the backbone. Remove the belly lining; on a fish that has been frozen, it can taste rancid. Place fillets skin-side down on foil on a broiler pan. Sprinkle lightly with garlic powder (not garlic salt), basil, and parsley. Broil fish without turning. When top begins to turn opaque, add ½ teaspoon lemon juice per fillet. Do not overcook. Spread fillets with butter just before serving.

Serves 4.

MUSSELS WITH PASTA

Mussels are a tasty bonus for those willing to make the effort to search them out along the rocky New England shoreline. If you're not so inclined, you can "harvest" them at your favorite fishmonger's.

1 quart shucked mussels, with juice	4 to 5 sprigs fresh parsley, chopped
Butter, for frying	1 teaspoon dried sweet basil
½ cup olive oil	1 teaspoon horseradish, or more to taste
1 onion, coarsely chopped	1 cup tomato juice or crushed tomatoes
2 stalks celery, diced	8 to 10 ounces spinach pasta twists or spinach noodles
2 large cloves garlic, minced (or substitute ½ teaspoon garlic powder)	¼ cup mixed grated Parmesan and Romano cheese
1 red sweet bell pepper, chopped	
1 large green pepper, chopped	

Prepare mussels by removing them from their juice and stir-frying briefly in a small amount of butter until cooked but not tough. Reserve juice to add to sauce. (If you have foraged your own mussels, scrub the shells well and steam the mussels in a small amount of water until all the shells have opened. Carefully pour the juice into a quart jar, straining it if necessary to avoid including sand. Pick out the mussels and stir-fry briefly in butter as above.)

Heat olive oil in a large iron skillet. Add onion, celery, garlic, red pepper, and green pepper, and sauté until vegetables are soft. Add parsley, basil, and horseradish; add tomato juice (or crushed tomatoes) and enough reserved mussel liquid to make a juicy sauce for the pasta. Heat through and add mussels at the very end (the vegetables should keep their shape, and the mussels should not be overcooked). Cook pasta *al dente*, drain, and place in a medium-sized oblong baking dish or shallow casserole. Spoon on mussels and vegetables, and sprinkle with grated cheese. Toss and serve. Note: Vegetables for this dish may be varied to taste. Fennel makes an interesting addition; in season, fresh peas, green beans, tomatoes, zucchini, and other garden vegetables may be used.

Serves 4 to 6.

SNUFF-BOX DUCK

This is an elegant dish for a special occasion. The buttermilk removes the strong taste often found in sea ducks, leaches out bloodshot game birds, and also acts as a tenderizer. Alex uses only crockery, stainless steel, or glass containers in this recipe, never aluminum.

1½ pounds duck breasts
2 to 4 cups buttermilk
½ pound bacon
2 cloves garlic, crushed
1 medium onion,
　chopped
1 medium green pepper,
　chopped

2 stalks celery, diced
½ cup flour
½ teaspoon dried basil
½ teaspoon dried
　parsley
Orange marmalade

Marinate duck in buttermilk for 24 hours. Fry bacon in a heavy skillet; remove when crisp. Brown crushed garlic in hot bacon fat and remove when browned (do not burn). Add chopped onion, green pepper, and celery to hot fat. Sauté vegetables until soft. Dredge marinated duck breasts in flour seasoned with basil and parsley, and add to vegetable mix. Fry until edge of bottom side turns brown. Turn the breasts and cook until juices begin to appear through the top coating. Crumble crisp bacon on the breasts. Top each piece with 1 tablespoon of marmalade. Cover and let simmer for 5 to 6 minutes. Remove and serve on a bed of steamed wild or brown rice.

Serves 2 to 3.

BREADED VENISON (OR VEAL) CHOPS

This recipe features a delicate lightly seasoned coating, and comes from Alex's mother-in-law, Mary Buzek.

6 to 8 chops (loin chops preferred)	¼ teaspoon dried basil
½ cup vegetable oil	¼ teaspoon dried parsley
2 eggs	Dash or two of white pepper
2 tablespoons milk	2 cups crushed saltine crackers
¼ teaspoon garlic powder	

Wipe off chops with a damp cloth, making sure no bone dust remains from butchering. Heat oil in a large cast-iron skillet. Beat eggs and add milk. Combine spices with mortar and pestle to ensure a thorough blend; add to cracker crumbs and mix thoroughly. Dip chops into milk-and-egg mix, then into crumb-spice mixture. Fry chops over medium heat until coating is medium brown; they will be cooked but still moist inside. *Serves 6 to 8.*

BAKED VEAL FLANK

A tasty way to serve a less-than-prime cut of meat. Also works well with venison and lamb. Let meat cool slightly before carving, and use a well-sharpened knife.

1 veal flank with ribs	½ teaspoon basil
¼ cup chopped raisins	½ teaspoon parsley
½ cup milk	¼ cup chopped black
2 cups bread crumbs	olives
1 large egg	½ pound cooked and
¼ teaspoon garlic	crumbled sausage
powder	

To remove ribs, cut along tissue line from outside edge of flank toward backbone. Resulting flank should look like an opened book. Allow raisins to "plump" in milk; then mix with remaining ingredients to make a stuffing. Distribute stuffing evenly on bottom half of flank. Place top half over stuffing. Coat outside of top half lightly with additional garlic powder, salt, and a light dusting of white pepper. Bake at 350° to 375°F. for 45 minutes. Serve with mint jelly or cranberry sauce. *Serves 6.*

BLADE STEAKS WITH SALT PORK SPREAD

This salt pork spread is also excellent on venison steaks.

1 (2-inch) cube salt pork
3 tablespoons chopped
  fresh parsley
2 cloves fresh garlic,
  minced, or ½
  teaspoon garlic
  powder

4 boneless chuck top
  blade steaks

On a cutting board, mince the salt pork with a sharp chef's knife until it becomes pastelike. Add the parsley and garlic and continue to mince, folding and cutting so that the paste turns green (add more parsley if necessary). Place steaks on a broiler pan and spread the tops with the salt pork mixture. Broil steaks; then turn and spread with more of the salt pork and continue broiling until the steaks are of the desired doneness. (The amount of cooking time will vary with the thickness of the steak.)   *Serves 4 to 6.*

ALEX'S CHEESECAKE

Alex's recipe for this elegant, smooth cheesecake (more like a torte, Alex says) is the one most often requested by his friends.

2 tablespoons butter
4 zwieback, grated
4 egg whites
1 cup sugar, plus 2
  tablespoons for
  topping

3 packages (8 ounces
  each) cream cheese,
  softened
  (Philadelphia
  preferred)
1½ teaspoons vanilla
2 cups sour cream
Generous amount of
  fresh fruit for topping

Using the 2 tablespoons of butter, generously butter an 8-inch spring-form cake pan. Dust with zwieback crumbs and shake out excess. Beat egg whites until they are fairly stiff, but not as stiff as for meringue. Add 1 cup sugar gradually, beating until blended. Add the softened cream cheese and beat until smooth. Add 1 teaspoon vanilla and blend in, beating for 1 or 2 minutes. Pour the batter into the spring-form pan. Bake in a 350°F. oven for about 30 minutes, until small cracks begin to appear. Blend sour cream with remaining 2 tablespoons sugar and remaining ½ teaspoon vanilla, and pour on top of cheesecake. Return to oven and bake for 5 minutes at 475°. The cake is set when bubbles form at the edge. Remove from oven and let cool in pan. Refrigerate for at least 2 hours before removing sides of pan. To serve, top with your favorite fresh fruit, passing additional fruit on the side; sliced strawberries are an especially attractive topping.

Makes ample for 10.

Richard Travisano at work in his kitchen.

Making the Most of "Found" Food

RICHARD TRAVISANO
Wakefield, Rhode Island

Richard Travisano is a self-taught cook who has, over count-less meals, evolved into a mine of expertise on the art of preparing "found" food. Sometimes this found food is the game birds he shoots or friends donate; other times it is the oysters, clams, and mussels he harvests from nearby Narragansett Bay; and, on occasion, it is even the various wild beasts and birds that wander into his backyard. However, it is the preparation of the wild game birds that is Richard's forte and culinary love.

"The secret to cooking these wild birds," Richard says, "is to pretend they're beef, and roast them until they are medium rare. The meat should be pink and juicy. And," he continues, "because wild birds, especially young ones, have less fat than supermarket fowl, you sometimes have to lard them." To accomplish this, Richard either inserts strips of fat with an old-fashioned larding needle or bastes the birds liberally with butter.

The pleasure Richard gets from preparing (and eating) the birds is almost as great as the satisfaction he reaps from turning the picked-over bones into soups worthy of coronation. As is clear from the sample here — "Pheasant Soup Sweeney" — in Richard's hands, the making of these soups is indeed an art.

If, as he puts it, he can ever stop experimenting with his recipes long enough to write them down, and can spare the time from his work in sociology, Richard plans to complete a cookbook. Fortunately, we don't have to wait for the book; Richard has written out a few of his recipes for us to try.

113

PHEASANT SOUP SWEENEY

Richard concocted this soup in honor of Jim Sweeney of Watertown, Connecticut — a hunting partner. The pheasant remains are reroasted to give the soup a rich brown color. The recipe is time-consuming, but the end result is worth it.

Remains of 1 baked pheasant
Small piece of cooked beef (such as a steak bone or leftover steak meat)
2 ounces dark sesame oil
5 to 7 ounces amontillado sherry or 3 to 5 ounces sweeter grade
Black pepper to taste
½ cup dry white wine
Water as needed
4 medium leeks
¼ teaspoon tarragon
¼ teaspoon chervil
2 pinches basil
8 to 10 chicken hearts and/or gizzards
2 large cloves garlic
Olive oil
Butter
Salt to taste
2 large slices crusty French bread
4 to 6 slices hard Gruyère cheese
4 to 6 slices Monastery cheese (Richard prefers Bauemstolz from Austria)

Paint the remains of the pheasant and the steak bone with a mixture of most of the sesame oil and 2 ounces of the sherry. Grind black pepper liberally over all and roast at 350°F., basting every few minutes with white wine, until very brown. Add water to avoid burning the juices, and use the broiler, if needed, to finish the job. Place in a soup pot and add 2 medium leeks (sliced, leaves and all), tarragon, chervil, and basil. Cover with water; add scrapings from baking pan or broiler, and bring to a boil. Slice the chicken hearts, gizzards, and garlic, and sauté them in a little olive oil, butter, and an ounce or so of the remaining sherry until well browned. Add to soup. Scrape the pan clean, swirl it with water, and add the liquid to the soup pot. Simmer, covered, at medium heat (adding water as necessary) for 3 to 4 hours, until everything is thoroughly simmered. Strain first through a colander (pressing with a wooden spoon) and then through cheesecloth. Return to a clean pot and bring to a boil. Reduce the stock to about 16 ounces. When it is close to fully condensed, adjust seasonings with salt, pepper, and more sherry: the taste you are after is rich and complex. Then refrigerate stock until ready to use.

To finish the soup, slice the 2 remaining leeks thinly up to the leaves and sauté well in a little olive oil and a bit more sesame oil. Bring the stock to a simmer and pour into two 12-ounce ovenproof soup dishes. Sprinkle the surface with a pinch of tarragon, and place a slice of good French bread (dry the bread first by toasting it in a slow oven) on top. Add a layer of sliced Gruyère cheese and a layer of sliced Monastery cheese. Bake at 400°F. until cheese melts, and then brown under the broiler. Serve at once. Note: This recipe can be closely approximated by using about half the bones and remains of a 12- to 14-pound turkey instead of the pheasant.

Makes 2 hearty servings.

ROAST PHEASANT

This unpretentious bird, cajoled into tenderness and taste by bastings of wine and garlic, and plumped out with a buttery cornbread stuffing, adds a holiday aura to any meal.

¼ pound sweet butter
1 pheasant, with giblets
¾ cup chopped fresh
  mushrooms
Black pepper as needed
Garlic powder as
  needed
Ground thyme as
  needed
1½ cups dry white wine,
  more or less
4 stalks celery, with
  leaves, diced (about 2
  cups)

¼ cup chicken stock
1 package Thomas's
  Corn Toast-R-Cakes
Several garlic cloves,
  minced
Tarragon
Water as needed
Richard's Sauce Seven
  (recipe follows)
Fine-quality red jelly

Melt 3 ounces of butter in a heavy skillet. Add diced pheasant giblets (and/or chicken giblets, to total ½ cup). Sauté well. Add chopped mushrooms, about ½ teaspoon black pepper, a pinch or two garlic powder, a dusting of thyme, and an ounce or two of white wine. Sauté well. Add celery and sauté for 5 minutes. Add chicken stock; bring to a boil and set aside to cool. Cut corn cakes in small cubes to make about 2 cups. Toast well in an oven. Mix these into the giblets mixture. The idea is to soak up the butter and stock: the mixture should be on the dry side, as the bird will be juicy.

Wash the pheasant inside and out with cold water and dry well. Pour about 2 ounces of white wine into the cavity, roll it around, and let it drip out. Dust the cavity with more black pepper and garlic powder. Stuff the bird with the corn mixture and truss it up. Tie the legs to the tail and the wings to the body. Rub the bird with more black pepper, part of the minced garlic, and the rest of the butter. Place in a heavy roasting pan. Place the bird in a preheated 400°F. oven for 10 minutes, then reduce the heat to 350°. Pheasants and other game birds are low on fat, so be careful not to burn the drippings. Bring 1 cup of white wine, 2 pinches of tarragon, and the rest of the garlic to a boil to make a basting sauce. Baste frequently with this mixture and with the pan drippings. Add water if necessary. A 2½-pound pheasant takes about 1½ hours to cook. The bird is done when clear juices (not red) run generously when you cut into the breast along the bone. Do not let the bird dry out.

When the bird is done, remove it from the oven and set aside on a warmed platter. Working quickly, add a bit of water to the pan drippings and stir around over low heat. Adjust the seasoning with pepper and white wine. The gravy will be tasty but a bit thin. Add spoonfuls of Richard's Sauce Seven carefully, tasting after each addition. Add a spoonful or two of jelly and stir well. Carve the bird and serve the sauce in a gravy boat. *Serves 2.*

RICHARD'S SAUCE SEVEN

Richard always has at least a little of this versatile sauce in his refrigerator. He not only uses it to perk up his roast pheasant, but also includes it in many of his soups and gravies.

Poultry necks, giblets, or leftovers equaling the bulk of the neck and giblets from a 12- to 14-pound turkey	4 ounces Madeira, more or less
	1 large onion, sliced
	1 large carrot, thinly sliced
Small amount of darker meat (goose, duck, or even beef)	1 tablespoon parsley
	1 teaspoon mushroom soy sauce
2 tablespoons olive oil	1 teaspoon basil
1 tablespoon butter	1 bay leaf
2 cloves garlic, sliced	1 stalk celery, with leaves, chopped
2 shallots, sliced	Large pinch marjoram
2 teaspoons black pepper, more or less to taste	Salt to taste

In a heavy kettle, sauté the meat pieces thoroughly with olive oil, butter, sliced garlic cloves, sliced shallots, liberal amount of the black pepper, and Madeira. When well browned, add onion, carrot, parsley, mushroom soy sauce, basil, bay leaf, celery, marjoram, and salt. Cover with water and simmer for 2 or 3 hours. Strain and reduce over low heat to 8 to 12 ounces, adjusting seasoning with more pepper, Madeira, and perhaps a bit more mushroom soy sauce. The sauce will keep in a jar in the refrigerator for at least several weeks. *Yield: ½ to ¾ pint.*

BAKED OYSTERS WITH TRIPLE CREME

Once the oysters are shucked and cleaned, this is an easy recipe — and a deliciously elegant one. Can be served as an appetizer as well as a main dish.

16 medium to large oysters (choose oysters of similar size to ensure equal cooking)
Black pepper to taste
Garlic powder to taste
Whole wheat crackers, crushed (about ½ cup)
2 ounces sherry

2 ounces lemon juice
1 cup finely chopped fresh mushrooms
French L'Explorateur cheese (Brillat Savarin or any other double- or triple-creme cheese will do, as long as it is mild)
Paprika, for dusting

Shuck oysters into a bowl; reserve liquor for oyster stew. Arrange empty shells in a baking pan, propping them up with rock salt or extra shells. Season the shells lightly with black pepper and garlic powder; place oysters in shells and season similarly. Sprinkle the oysters with cracker crumbs. Combine the sherry and lemon juice and steep mushrooms in the mixture for a few minutes. Then spoon mushrooms onto the oysters. Top each oyster with a dollop of cheese. Dust with paprika and bake at 400°F. for 20 to 25 minutes. These oysters are tastiest when moist but not too juicy.

Serves 2, teases 4.

THE RIGHT RICE

This rice has a lovely delicate flavor, made all the nicer with the addition of the crunchy walnuts. A welcome new rice dish.

1 cup long-grain (brown or white) rice
4 to 5 ounces butter
1½ cups good chicken stock
1 large pinch saffron
2 large pinches paprika
2 pinches cumin
4 to 5 dashes mushroom soy sauce, or as needed
8 ounces fresh mushrooms, sliced

1 tablespoon or so olive oil
Garlic powder to taste
Black pepper to taste
1 to 2 ounces dry red wine
1 ounce Madeira
4 ounces walnut meats, cut in small pieces (not chopped)
2 to 3 tablespoons sour cream

Wash the rice in water once or twice, then drain and set aside. Melt 2 ounces of the butter in a skillet and sauté the rice for 3 to 5 minutes. In a saucepan you can cover tightly, bring the stock to a boil. Add saffron, paprika, and cumin, as well as a dash or two of mushroom soy sauce, if the stock is not salted. Add the rice, return it to a boil, and simmer, covered, over low heat for about 20 minutes, until all liquid is absorbed. Sauté the mushrooms in 2 to 3 ounces of butter and a bit of olive oil, seasoning them with a dash or two garlic powder, black pepper, red wine, Madeira, and a few dashes of mushroom soy sauce. Add the walnut meats and sauté for an additional 4 minutes. Set this aside.

When the rice is done, stir in 2 to 3 tablespoons of sour cream — enough to make it sticky. Gently stir three-quarters of the mushroom mixture into the rice. Put the rice into 4 small au gratin dishes (or one big one) and put the rest of the mushrooms on top. Bake at 400°F. for 8 to 10 minutes, and you have the right rice. *Serves 4 to 5.*

SHREDDED ZUCCHINI

This is a tasty thing to do with the zucchini so plentiful in the summertime. But a warning: don't take shortcuts with the salting and squeezing, or it will be too moist.

2 medium zucchini
Salt as needed
1 medium onion
½ teaspoon garlic
  powder
½ teaspoon onion
  powder
Black pepper to taste
1 tablespoon grated
  Romano or Parmesan
  cheese, or more to
  taste

Freshly grated nutmeg
½ stick sweet butter
1 large clove garlic,
  minced
Grated mozzarella to
  taste

Grate 2 medium zucchini into a large bowl, skin and all (with large zucchini, remove the seeds first). Salt the zucchini liberally and let sit for at least 20 minutes. Flood the bowl with water and strain. Repeat the bath 2 or 3 times until the salt is fully washed out. Flood the zucchini again and squeeze handfuls as hard as you can between your palms. Peel and grate a medium onion into the bowl with the zucchini. Fluff and mix with a fork. Add garlic powder, onion powder, black pepper, 1½ teaspoons of grated Romano (or Parmesan) cheese, and a medium sprinkling of nutmeg. Mix with a fork. In a saucepan, melt butter and lightly sauté the garlic. Remove pan from heat. Toss the zucchini mixture into the pan and stir. Divide the zucchini into 4 au gratin dishes and cover lightly with grated mozzarella and a bit more grated Romano (or Parmesan). Bake at 400°F. for 5 minutes, then brown the cheese under the broiler. *Serves 4.*

Deborah Abbott Kennard puts the finishing touches on her lamb dinner.

Lamb From Wellscroft Farm

DEBORAH ABBOTT KENNARD
Chesham, New Hampshire

The New England cooks we have met so far are not alone in their resolve to make the most of what's at hand: Deborah Kennard and her husband, David, join them. However, the Kennards don't "find" their food as Richard Travisano and Alex Delicata often do, nor do they catch it or grow it as others do — they raise it.

It all began with Solomon and Sheba, two sheep the Kennards bought in the spring of 1974 with high hopes of reintroducing successful sheep farming to the sprawling pastures of Wellscroft Farm, their home in the southwestern corner of New Hampshire. Their hopes were well met: thanks to Sheba and her mate, and the many more that followed, the Kennards now find themselves the richer for a thriving flock of more than 200 breeding ewes, as well as from many delicious lamb meals enjoyed over the years.

An important part of the Kennards' efforts to help promote sheep farming in the region is their work to educate the general public to the proper and frequent use of lamb. (To some who have not always met the fine young lamb now available, a lamb dinner remains not always a happy memory.) To meet this goal — as well as to enhance their own eating pleasure — Deborah works diligently in her small farm kitchen (once the woodshed, privy, and cider mill of their 1773 farmhouse) to master the preparation of lamb dishes and to develop tempting lamb recipes and helpful cooking information to disseminate to area markets and food-news outlets. Her rules for lamb cookery are simple: (1) remove the fell (outer membrane); (2) remove the excess fat (lamb fat is "hard" fat and

123

burns easily); and (3) do not overcook lamb ("It is best," Deborah says, "on the rare side"). Her recipes, as you'll find when you try them, are excellent, and varied — proof positive that lamb should no longer be relegated only to the occasional company roast or the traditional Easter dinner. Sheba and her descendants may not be happy that Deborah's work is going so well, but the rest of us should be.

ROAST LEG OF LAMB

The coating for Deborah's roast leg of lamb is based on one of Julia Child's in her Mastering the Art of French Cooking. *It both seals in the juices and adds a delightful flavor. If at all possible, use the fresh rosemary.*

1 (6-pound) leg of lamb
½ cup Dijon-type
   prepared mustard
2 tablespoons soy sauce
1 clove garlic, mashed
1 teaspoon ground
   rosemary or thyme
   (or 1 tablespoon
   fresh, chopped)

¼ teaspoon powdered
   ginger
2 tablespoons olive oil

Be sure to remove the fell or filament and all excess fat from the lamb. Blend the mustard, soy sauce, garlic, herbs, and ginger in a bowl. Beat in the olive oil drop by drop to make a mayonnaise-like coating. Using a rubber spatula or brush, paint the lamb with the mixture and set it on the rack of a roasting pan. (For best flavor, coat the meat several hours before roasting.) Roast at 300°F. for 10 to 12 minutes per pound for medium rare (bone in), 13 to 15 minutes per pound for well done. Do not exceed a meat-thermometer reading of 155° to 160°, or the meat will lose much of its juice and flavor. For a boned leg, the cooking time more than doubles.

Serves 6 generously, 8 less so.

LAMB RIBLETS

This flavorful, easy-to-prepare lamb dish makes room for one of the several tangy home-brewed marinades Deborah has developed.

2½ pounds lamb riblets
  (figure 3 or 4 per
  serving)

1 recipe Curry or Kebab
  Marinade (recipes
  follow)

Parboil riblets for 20 to 30 minutes to remove the superficial fat to make the ribs crispier when they're done. Remove from liquid and marinate in your choice of marinades overnight, turning riblets to be sure they are well coated with marinade. Preheat oven to 300°F. Arrange riblets in baking pan, baste with marinade, and bake until tender, 25 to 30 minutes. Baste frequently while baking. *Serves 4.*

CURRY MARINADE

This marinade has a strong, rich flavor curry fans will love.

¾ cup soy sauce
1 clove garlic, crushed
1 tablespoon curry
  powder

½ teaspoon grated fresh
  ginger (you can
  substitute powdered
  ginger in a pinch)

Mix all ingredients together and pour over meat. Marinate for 2 hours at room temperature or overnight in refrigerator.

Makes ¾ cup.

KEBAB MARINADE

For a blander marinade, cut the soy and Worcestershire sauces a bit.

1 cup red wine
½ cup soy sauce
1 cup pineapple juice
1 teaspoon dried thyme
1 teaspoon dried
  rosemary

¼ cup Worcestershire
  sauce
1 onion, finely chopped
Grating of fresh black
  pepper

Mix all ingredients together and pour over meat. Marinate for 2 hours at room temperature or overnight in refrigerator.

Makes 2 to 3 cups.

LAMB STEW WITH YOGURT

This lightly seasoned stew allows the vegetables and slightly tart yogurt to shine through.

1 tablespoon butter
1½ pounds boneless
    lamb stew meat (2
    pounds with bone in)
1 teaspoon salt
¾ teaspoon dried dill
    weed (1½ to 2
    teaspoons fresh dill
    preferred)
2 cups water

4 or 5 medium potatoes,
    peeled and quartered
4 or 5 carrots, peeled
    and cut in 2-inch
    pieces
3 or 4 stalks celery, cut
    in 2-inch pieces
1 cup plain yogurt
2 tablespoons flour

Melt butter in a large (5-quart) heavy pot and brown meat on all sides. Add salt, dill weed, and water. Cover and simmer for about 1 hour, until meat is almost tender. Add potatoes, carrots, and celery and simmer for an additional 30 minutes, until vegetables are tender. In a small bowl, combine yogurt and flour with a whisk. Remove meat and vegetables to a warmed serving dish and add yogurt mixture to liquid in pan. Cook over low heat, stirring constantly, until thickened; then cook 2 minutes longer. Pour gravy over lamb and vegetables. *Serves 4.*

LAMB SALAD

A tasty and eye-appealing summertime use for leftover lamb.

⅔ cup olive oil or vegetable oil

¼ cup red wine vinegar

1 tablespoon freshly squeezed lemon juice

2 teaspoons Dijon-style mustard

¾ teaspoon dried oregano, crumbled

¼ teaspoon salt

3 drops hot pepper sauce

1 clove garlic, peeled and minced

2 cups cooked, cubed lamb

1 bunch broccoli, blanched and cut into florets

½ pound (about 3 cups) mushrooms, sliced

2 small red sweet peppers, seeded and cut into strips

Leaf lettuce

Chopped fresh basil or parsley, for garnish

In a small bowl, combine oil, vinegar, lemon juice, mustard, oregano, salt, hot pepper sauce, and garlic. In a large bowl, combine lamb, broccoli, mushrooms, and peppers. Toss lamb and vegetables with dressing. Serve on a bed of lettuce and sprinkle with chopped basil or parsley. Note: Other vegetables may be added as desired, including blanched julienned carrots; blanched, sliced, or julienned zucchini or yellow squash; tomato wedges; and steamed brussels sprouts. *Serves 4.*

SUMMERHOUSE LAMB SALAD

A colorful and intriguing salad combination.

2 cups slivered cooked
lamb
1 can (15¼ ounces)
kidney beans, drained
1 large tart apple, cored
and cubed
1 medium cucumber,
peeled, seeded, and
sliced
¼ cup chopped
scallions
½ cup vegetable oil

3 tablespoons lemon
juice
1 teaspoon curry
powder
½ teaspoon ground
cumin
½ teaspoon salt
Lettuce
½ cup broken walnuts
(optional)

In a medium bowl, combine lamb, kidney beans, apple, cucumber, and scallions. In a small bowl, combine oil, lemon juice, curry powder, cumin, and salt. Pour over lamb and mix well. Chill for several hours, stirring occasionally. To serve, spoon onto lettuce leaves and sprinkle with walnuts if desired. *Serves 4.*

LAMB EGG ROLLS

A fun idea for leftover lamb. Almost any combination of vegetables will work: just keep a proportion of two or three times vegetables to lamb. A nice bonus: this recipe will work well with other meats, too, especially chicken, and just as well with only vegetables.

In a wok or skillet, cook a clove of garlic in vegetable oil; remove and discard garlic. Finely mince some onion, carrot, broccoli, Chinese cabbage, or other vegetables, and quickly stir-fry. Remove vegetables with a slotted spoon. Add ½ to 1 cup of leftover cooked rice, and about the same quantity of bean sprouts. Finely chop leftover lamb and add to mixture. Mix well. Add 1 beaten egg to bind the mixture. Place a generous tablespoonful in the center of each egg roll wrapper (available in supermarkets) and fold up the wrapper envelope-style, sealing with a mixture of 1 teaspoon cornstarch in ¼ cup water. Fry in hot vegetable oil in a wok, turning to brown the rolls evenly. Drain on brown paper and keep rolls warm in oven until ready to serve.

Makes 1 dozen to 2 dozen, depending on amount of stuffing made.

ZUCCHINI FESTIVAL LAMB KEBABS

A nice change-of-pace crowd pleaser — something to think about the next time you or your favorite organization is faced with feeding a mob.

150 pounds lamb, cubed
1 gallon olive oil
1 gallon burgundy
1 quart wine vinegar
12 lemons, grated and juiced
3 large bulbs garlic, pressed
3 to 4 tablespoons salt to taste
1 to 2 tablespoons freshly ground pepper

3 tablespoons oregano
20 to 30 pounds onions, skinned and cut into 1¼-inch chunks
20 to 30 pounds green peppers, cut in 1½-inch strips
20 to 30 pounds cherry tomatoes

Combine all ingredients except lamb and vegetables in a large clean tub or other container. Add lamb and marinate for at least 24 hours. Alternate lamb cubes on skewers with chunks of onion, green pepper, and cherry tomatoes. Grill, basting with marinade.

Yield: approximately 450 kebabs.

PILAF

This pilaf has a slightly nutty flavor that is a perfect complement to Deborah's good lamb dishes.

¼ cup butter
¼ to ½ cup finely
  chopped scallions,
  shallots, or chives
½ teaspoon finely
  chopped garlic
½ cup (approximately)
  very thin egg noodles

1 cup raw rice
2 cups chicken broth
  (don't skimp; it needs
  the moisture)
Salt as needed

Melt butter in a heavy 2-quart saucepan; add the scallions and garlic and cook briefly, stirring continuously. Add the noodles and stir over low heat for about 3 minutes. Add the rice and cook for 5 minutes, still stirring. In another pan, bring the broth to a full boil and add it all at once to the rice mixture. (If the broth is not salty enough, add salt to taste.) Cover the saucepan tightly and let pilaf simmer for 35 minutes. Do not remove the cover. Turn off the heat and let rice stand, covered, for 10 to 20 minutes before serving.

Serves 4.

FRESH MINT JELLY

This is, of course, the traditional accompaniment for lamb — and oh, so good!

1 cup fresh mint leaves and stems, firmly packed	3½ cups sugar
	4 drops green food coloring
½ cup apple cider vinegar	3 ounces (½ bottle) liquid fruit pectin
1 cup water	

Wash the mint, but do not remove the leaves from the stems. Drain, then place in a heavy saucepan. Bruise the mint with the bottom of a heavy glass tumbler. Add vinegar, water, and sugar, and bring to a full, rolling boil over high heat, stirring until the sugar melts. Add the coloring and pectin and return to a full boil, stirring constantly. Boil hard for 30 seconds. Remove from heat, and skim. Pour through a fine sieve into hot sterilized jelly glasses. Seal. *Makes about 2 pints.*

QUICK MINT SAUCE

Many prefer a fresh mint sauce to jelly for their lamb. This simple and well-flavored sauce fills the bill nicely.

Dissolve 1½ tablespoons confectioners' sugar in 3 table-spoons hot water. Let cool. Add ½ cup vinegar of choice, and ⅓ cup chopped fresh mint leaves. Let steep for a short while, then serve warm or cool. *Yield: approximately ¾ cup.*

Ruth Baird relaxing in her strawberry patch.

1,500 Jars of Jellies and Jams
... And More

RUTH BAIRD
Lancaster, Massachusetts

It would be hard to imagine a book on New England cookery without sure-fire recipes for jellies, jams, and butters. Long lines of these preserves along pantry shelves are almost as much a part of the New England landscape as the long lines of stone walls along its roadways. And Ruth Baird does her share: each summer she "puts up" something akin to 1,500 jars of these sure-to-sell favorites for a local farm stand — in addition, of course, to those she puts up for her own family.

Almost as much in demand by the farm stand customers are her freely dispensed hints for success. Here are a few: (1) use Sure-Jell (Ruth's preference) for jellies, and follow the directions; (2) never pick strawberries when they're wet (they get mushy); (3) if you're short on time, freeze the juice from the fruits and make the jellies later; (4) never try to save time by doubling up on batches of jam and jelly (the sugar can crystallize and the batch may not thicken); (5) don't keep wax-sealed jars in a cold place (the wax may contract and slip away from the jar); and (6) when making jam, butter the kettle rim so the jam won't boil over.

But making jams and jellies is not all that Ruth and her husband, John, accomplish on their three-acre Massachusetts homestead. A quick tour reveals the source of all the food needed to fill their three freezers, dozens of canning jars, and the fruit cellar under their home. Off to one side is a small grove of dwarf fruit trees (Ruth prefers the dwarf varieties because they are compact and yield in a shorter time). There's also a raised-bed garden and a small greenhouse, blueberry and raspberry bushes, and — of course — a strawberry bed. As you leaf through Ruth's recipes, you'll see where much of this produce goes.

In addition, the Bairds raise at least one steer ("We only break even") and two pigs ("We come out a little ahead on the pork") a year. It's no wonder that Ruth says with some pride that they "often put a meal on the table that's completely produced on our farm" — a meal no doubt enhanced by at least one of her many jars of jellies and jams.

APPLE BUTTER

This butter is lovely spread on toast, exquisite on vanilla ice cream, and an excellent use for the fall's excess apple bounty.

10 pounds apples (use a mixture of varieties for good flavor)	Sugar
	1 teaspoon cinnamon
	½ teasoon allspice
1 cup water	½ teaspoon cloves
2 cups cider	¼ teaspoon salt

Core but do not peel apples. Cut up apples and place them in a large kettle with the water and cider. Cook mixture until apples are soft, then put through a food mill. Place mixture in a pan and cook down for about 25 minutes, stirring to keep from scorching. Then measure the pulp, and for every 3 cups of pulp add 1 cup of sugar (or less for a tarter butter). Add spices and salt, and cook, stirring frequently, until butter is thick. Pour into hot sterilized canning jars and seal.   *Makes about 6 pints.*

VARIATION: A quick way to make the butter without constant stirring is to cook the mixture uncovered in a roasting pan in a 250°F. oven for about 3 hours. Stir a couple of times, and when the butter is at the desired consistency, spoon it into hot sterilized canning jars and seal.

PEAR BUTTER

Pear butter makes a pleasant change-of-pace spread. It, too, can be made by the quicker apple butter process.

Peel and core pears and put them through a food chopper (or chop by hand). Cook in own juice at a simmer for about 30 minutes to reduce. Measure pulp, and for every 3 cups of pulp add 1 cup sugar. Add seasonings to taste: about ½ teaspoon nutmeg, 1 teaspoon cinnamon, and ½ teaspoon salt for every batch (adjust seasonings for larger amount of fruit). Cook in a heavy kettle on top of stove until butter is very thick (almost holding its shape) and isn't watery around the edges. Stir often to keep from burning. Pack into hot sterilized jars and seal; process in a boiling-water bath for about 10 minutes if desired.   *10 pounds makes 4 to 5 pints.*

PEACH BUTTER: Proceed by same method. Spice with ginger.

PEACH JAM

Ruth finds a food mill indispensable in preparing this jam.

5 cups peach purée (10 to 15 large peaches)	½ teaspoon cloves (optional)
6 cups sugar	½ teaspoon allspice (optional)
Juice and rind of 1 lemon	

Remove pits and imperfect parts from peaches. In a large kettle, simmer peaches with just enough water to keep them from burning. When peaches are softened, put them through a food mill. Add sugar, lemon juice and rind, and spices, and cook slowly until thickened. Test for doneness by putting a spoonful on a plate. The jam should just hold its shape. Pour into hot sterilized jars and seal with paraffin.   *Yield: about 4 pints.*

PEAR MARMALADE

This marmalade scorches easily, so keep the heat low and watch the mixture carefully.

4 cups pear purée	3 cups sugar
Grated rind and juice of	
2 oranges	

Peel and core pears. Put them through the coarse blade of a food chopper and measure out 4 cups. Add orange rind and juice; then add sugar. Cook slowly until mixture is thickened as desired. Pour into hot sterilized jars and seal with paraffin. *Makes about 3 pints.*

HOT DOG RELISH

This is a simple and inexpensive way to "put by" a good share of your family's relish supply.

4 quarts green tomatoes	1 teaspoon mixed
2 onions	pickling spices
4 green peppers	3 cups vinegar
¼ head cabbage	1 cup water
½ cup salt	2 cups sugar

Wash vegetables and put them through the coarse blade of a food chopper. Add salt and let stand for several hours. Drain liquid from vegetables; discard liquid. Tie the spices in a cloth bag, and combine with vegetables, vinegar, water, and sugar in a large kettle. Simmer for 30 minutes. Remove cloth bag. Seal relish in hot sterilized jars. *Makes about 10 half-pints.*

HAMBURG-SAUSAGE BAKE

This is a favorite Baird family supper dish and, happily, an undemanding one.

1 pound ground pork
   sausage
2 pounds lean ground
   beef
2 cups mashed potatoes
1 medium onion,
   chopped
2 slices stale bread,
   crumbled

½ teaspoon thyme
½ teaspoon basil
½ teaspoon salt
½ teaspoon coarsely
   ground pepper
1 teaspoon sage

Brown pork sausage and beef; drain excess fat. Add mashed potatoes, onion, bread, and seasonings. Cook over low heat, stirring occasionally to keep from burning; taste and adjust seasoning if desired. Bake, covered, for about 25 minutes at 350°F. This can also be used as a turkey stuffing. *Serves 6 to 8.*

JELLY ROLL

A good recipe to help use up at least some of the hundreds of jars of jelly and jam Ruth puts up each summer and fall — and yours as well.

4 eggs
¾ cup sugar
¾ cup flour
¾ teaspoon baking
  powder
¼ teaspoon salt
1 teaspoon orange
  extract

1 tablespoon
  confectioners' sugar
1 cup homemade jelly,
  more or less as
  needed (preferably
  from a red berry)

Line a jelly-roll pan with waxed paper. Beat eggs until thick and creamy, then add sugar a little at a time. Combine dry ingredients and fold into egg mixture; add extract. Pour into jelly-roll pan and bake for 10 minutes at 350°F. Dust a clean dish towel with confectioners' sugar. Turn the baked jelly roll onto the towel and peel off the waxed paper. Do not let the cake cool too much before filling. Soften the jelly by beating with a fork. Then spread it lightly on the cake, starting from one end. Roll up the cake as you continue to spread the jelly. Dust with additional confectioners' sugar if desired. *Serves 8 to 10.*

BLUEBERRY TEA CAKE

Another simple-to-prepare Ruth Baird specialty, with a light texture and berries that stay in place.

2 tablespoons butter
1 cup granulated sugar,
  plus extra for
  sprinkling over top
2 eggs, separated
1½ cups flour

½ teaspoon baking
  powder
⅓ cup milk
1½ cups blueberries
Nutmeg

Cream butter and 1 cup sugar. Beat in egg yolks. Add flour and baking powder alternately with the milk. Fold in stiffly beaten egg whites, then lightly fold in blueberries. Spread batter in a greased 9-inch square pan. Sprinkle the top lightly with nutmeg and granulated sugar. Bake at 350°F. about 35 minutes or until top is light golden brown. *Yield: nine 3-inch squares.*

RUTH BAIRD'S STRAWBERRY SHORTCAKE

This spectacular shortcake is similar to Charlotte's Shortcake earlier in this collection, but Ruth uses Crisco instead of butter — and a lot more berries.

2 quarts berries	1 teaspoon salt
½ cup plus 2 tablespoons sugar	½ cup Crisco
2 cups flour	¾ cup milk, more or less
1 tablespoon baking powder	1 cup heavy cream, whipped

Wash and hull berries; set a few perfect ones aside for the garnish and cut up the rest. Add ½ cup sugar to the cut-up berries and set aside. Sift together flour, baking powder, salt, and the remaining 2 tablespoons sugar. Cut in Crisco until well mixed. Stirring quickly, add enough milk to make a soft dough. Turn out onto a floured board and — handling the dough as little as possible — shape into 2 rounds, each ½-inch thick and about 7 inches in diameter. Transfer to greased baking sheets and bake for 15 minutes at 400°F. Place 1 layer of hot biscuit on a serving platter and butter well. Spread with sugared berries. Top with second layer and more sugared berries. Add whipped cream and garnish with whole berries. Cut into wedges to serve. *Serves 8.*

Diana Prescott, blue ribbons in hand.

Blue Ribbon Recipes

DIANA PRESCOTT
Pembroke, New Hampshire

If pantry shelves heavy-laden with "put by" jams and jellies are one benchmark of the talented traditional New England cook, surely shelves lined row on row with tasty home-processed pickles must be another. Diana Prescott needn't worry: her choicest pickles claim a corner on the blue ribbons awarded each year at the Hopkinton (New Hampshire) Labor Day Fair.

And Diana doesn't stop at pickles. Anyone visiting the fair would most likely also find blue ribbons on a Prescott braided rug, on a beautiful rosemaled wooden box, and on several jars of golden honey (though, in fairness, the honey ribbons are actually the booty of Diana's husband, Stanley, the family's beekeeper).

Since the early days of their marriage when Diana "put up" her very first jelly in their first apartment, she and Stanley have sought to join the ranks of New England couples striving toward a nearly self-sufficient lifestyle. They have come a long way toward that goal. First, there are the gardens (one large family plot and four sub-plots, one for each of the children) from which Diana reaps the produce for her prize-winning pickles and for many of the family's "blue-ribbon" meals. Then, too, there is Jane, the Prescotts' gentle Jersey, and her offspring, Irwin and Dawn TGIF (born at sunrise on a Friday). Jane does her part by faithfully contributing a daily 1½ gallons of milk, including six cups of thick cream, from which Diana makes four pounds of butter weekly and uses the resulting buttermilk to make many of the family's baked goods ("Buttermilk makes them tenderer"). Meanwhile, Irwin and

141

Dawn TGIF graze languidly behind the barn as they await their turn to add to the Prescotts' freezer.

When asked what she'd like to add next to the Prescotts' self-sufficiency agenda, Diana is quick to reply, "A windmill . . . so we can say good-bye to the power company." Somehow, reviewing Diana's schedule as she goes through her blue-ribbon paces, one wonders why a windmill should be necessary: simply harnessing *her* energy should be enough!

CRISP PICKLE SLICES

The cucumbers for this prize-winning pickle are, of course, from the Prescotts' vegetable garden. Diana orders her long list of seeds from Vesey's Seeds of Prince Edward Island. Grown in Canada, Diana finds its Canadian-grown seeds the best for the short New Hampshire growing season.

4 quarts sliced unpeeled cucumbers (about ¼-inch thick)
6 onions, sliced
3 cloves garlic, peeled
⅓ cup pickling salt
5 cups sugar

3 cups cider vinegar
2 tablespoons mustard seed
1½ teaspoons turmeric
1½ teaspoons celery seed

Mix together cucumbers, onions, garlic, and pickling salt, and let stand overnight. Drain brine the next morning. In a large kettle, combine cucumbers with remaining ingredients. Bring to a boil; then pack in jars. Process for 5 minutes in a boiling-water bath.

Makes 4 quarts.

SOUR MUSTARD PICKLES

Another of Diana's prize-winning pickles.

1 gallon cider vinegar
1 cup uniodized
  pickling salt
¾ cup dry mustard
4 cups brown sugar
1 teaspoon alum
1 teaspoon turmeric

Enough 6-inch
  cucumbers,
quartered, to fill 8
quart jars (leave any
small cucumbers
whole)

Mix together vinegar, pickling salt, mustard, brown sugar, alum, and turmeric. Pack cucumbers on end in quart jars. Fill jars with the cold brine and let jars stand, covered, on a shelf for 3 or 4 days. Pour brine off into a large kettle and add additional cucumbers to jars wherever there's space. Heat the brine to boiling and pour over the cucumbers. Cover and process for 5 minutes in a boiling-water bath. *Makes 8 quarts.*

PICKLED BEETS

Pickled beets provide lively color as well as lively taste.

3 quarts cooked and
  peeled small beets
2 cups sugar
1½ teaspoons pickling
  salt
1 tablespoon whole
  allspice

3½ cups vinegar
1½ cups water
2 whole cinnamon
  sticks

To cook beets, wash and drain them, leaving 2 inches of stems and the taproots. Cover with boiling water and cook until tender. Set aside. Combine remaining ingredients and simmer for 15 minutes. Pack beets into jars, leaving ½-inch headspace, cutting large beets in half if necessary. Remove cinnamon sticks from brine. Bring brine to a boil and pour over beets, leaving ½-inch headspace. Cover and process for 30 minutes in a boiling-water bath.
Makes about 6 pints.

DILLY BEANS

When pickling beans, Diana recommends starting with white-seeded beans; brown-seeded beans will stain the water, a no-no for prize winning.

Enough green beans, trimmed (and snapped, if desired), to fill about 7 pint jars

2 heads of dill or 1 teaspoon dill seed for each jar

1 clove garlic for each jar

1 piece of hot red pepper or ¼ teaspoon crushed red pepper for each jar

¾ cup sugar

½ cup pickling salt

1 quart vinegar

1 quart water

3 tablespoons mixed pickling spices

Pack beans in jars, putting one dill head (or half the dill seed) at the bottom and the remaining dill at the top of each jar. Add a clove of garlic and a piece of red pepper (or the crushed red pepper) to each jar. Combine sugar, pickling salt, vinegar, and water. Tie spices in a cheesecloth bag and add to vinegar mixture. Simmer for 15 minutes. Remove spice bag. Heat brine to boiling and pour over packed beans, leaving ¼-inch headspace. Cover and process for 15 minutes in a boiling-water bath. *Makes 7 pints.*

SPLIT PEA SOUP

1 meaty ham bone	1 bay leaf
1 pound green split peas	2 or 3 peppercorns
1 onion, sliced	2 stalks celery, chopped
1 carrot, diced	

Using a large soup kettle, boil ham bone in water to cover, skimming off fat. Strain, reserving meat and broth. Cook peas and remaining ingredients in broth until soft, simmering gently for 2 to 3 hours. Remove bay leaf and put soup through a food mill to purée. Add pieces of ham; reheat and serve with cornbread.

Serves 5 to 6.

CHILI

Chili makes a wonderfully nutritious meat-stretching meal. This recipe makes a delicious, hearty one, and can be prepared in a Crockpot if you like. For a tamer chili, cut the chili powder a bit.

1 pound ground beef	⅛ teaspoon paprika
1 clove garlic	¼ teaspoon crushed red
2 green peppers,	pepper
chopped	½ teaspoon black
2 large onions, chopped	pepper
1 quart canned	2 bay leaves
tomatoes (or 2 to 3	1 large can (28 ounces)
pounds fresh)	baked kidney beans
2 teaspoons salt	(or other baked
2 tablespoons chili	beans)
powder	

Brown the ground beef in a small amount of oil. Add garlic, green peppers, and onions, and cook until onions are translucent. Next, add tomatoes (if using fresh tomatoes, remove the skins first). Then add all remaining ingredients except baked beans, and let simmer for 2 hours. Add beans and heat through.   *Serves 6.*

BLUE RIBBON WHEAT BREAD

This easy-to-make prize-winning bread is almost everybody's favorite — including the Prescotts, who especially like it with their chili suppers, except that it disappears too quickly!

2 cups water	3 cups whole wheat
2 cups milk	flour
½ cup honey	2 teaspoons salt
¼ cup molasses	2 eggs, beaten
3 scant tablespoons	5½ cups unbleached
active dry yeast	white flour

Combine water, milk, honey, and molasses in a saucepan and heat to 110° to 120°F. Add the yeast, and mix well until yeast is dissolved. In a large bowl, combine whole wheat flour and salt, then add the yeast mixture. Add eggs and beat batter with a wire whip until smooth. Begin adding white flour, stirring well, to make a soft dough (adding too much flour will create a heavy bread). Dough does not have to be kneaded. Cover bowl and let dough rise in a warm place until doubled. Spoon down and divide among 3 greased 5- by 9-inch loaf pans. Do not let dough rise again. Bake in a preheated 375°F. oven for 35 to 40 minutes, until loaves sound hollow when tapped. *Makes 3 loaves.*

WHITE BREAD

Another winner, and again, easy to make. The large yield provides enough to freeze some for later use.

3 cups scalded milk	2 packages (scant
6 tablespoons honey	tablespoon each)
1 tablespoon salt	active dry yeast
6 tablespoons butter	12 cups flour
1 cup cold water	

Scald milk and add honey, salt, and butter. Add cold water to cool the mixture. When mixture is lukewarm, add yeast and stir to dissolve. Add about 4 cups of the flour and stir with a wire whip until smooth. Gradually add 7 more cups of flour, mixing well. Turn out onto a board floured with the remaining 1 cup of flour and knead dough for 10 minutes, using minimal extra flour. Let rise in a greased bowl, covered, until doubled. Punch down, shape into loaves, and place in greased bread pans. Let rise again, then bake at 400°F. for 30 minutes or until loaves sound hollow when tapped.   *Makes 4 large or 6 smaller loaves.*

EASY YOGURT DESSERT

This is a lovely, light — not too disastrous to the waistline — dessert. Try the different gelatin flavors until you find the one you like best. Chances are, no matter which flavor you choose, you won't need much — if any — extra sweetener.

> 2 boxes flavored gelatin   Honey or sugar
> 1 cup boiling water   (optional)
> 4 cups yogurt

Dissolve gelatin in boiling water. Stir in yogurt and additional sweetening if desired. Pour into large dish or individual serving bowls, and chill until set.   *Serves 6 to 8.*

Jane Nordstrom in a favorite running shirt.

Good Food for Good Health

JANE NORDSTROM
Peru, Massachusetts

A more recent development in New England cookery is the turn, or maybe more accurately, return, to a more healthful, natural cuisine: cooking with whole grains, less fat, less salt, and unrefined sweeteners.

Jane Nordstrom happily embraces these practices. Always a serious cook (her Berkshire hillside kitchen has a six-burner range and a convection, as well as gas, oven), Jane is also a long-time author of a respected local newspaper food column. It wasn't until fairly recently, however, when ill health forced her to revamp her family's lifestyle, that Jane turned so enthusiastically to her present, more natural, cooking style. A seasoned bread baker and writer of two books on bread making, she now makes most of her breads without sugar ("There is sugar already present in the flour," she reminds us), shortening, or salt. Jane combines a small amount of yeast, water — preferably the vegetable or potato water she tries to keep on hand — and flour to make a sponge that allows a three-loaf batch of bread to rise beautifully. Another ingredient she keeps on hand for her bread making is a purée of cooked mixed vegetables (fresh in summer, frozen in winter), a cup or two of which she substitutes for some of the required liquid, adding color and flavor, as well as nutrition.

Jane also makes her own yogurt (rules for which follow in "Jane's Bread-Making Tips and Other Techniques"). This she uses whole in many ways, or drained thoroughly as a sour cream or cream cheese substitute, saving the whey for use in stock, in making rice, and in crêpe batter (as you'll find in her delicious recipe for spinach crêpes).

In addition to cutting salt from her bread and most meat from her diet, Jane's new lifestyle incorporates a rugged new running regimen — a regimen she has been following for about six years now, working up from her first very tentative one-tenth-mile jog on through six-mile and longer races, and more recently, to full-blown marathons. The running and the new cuisine have greatly improved her health and that of her husband, Carl — and Jane assures us, that despite rumors to the contrary from the running world, the running has not depressed her appetite. "Vanity and gluttony are the best reasons for running," she adds, laughing. And a good thing: it would be a pity not to be able to enjoy Jane's good food for good health.

ANCHOVY-WALNUT-YOGURT DIP

Hosts and hostesses are always looking for a distinctive dip to try. This combination of nuts, anchovies, and yogurt is certainly different, and very good. You might want to serve it with Jane's Four-Grain Crackers (recipe following later in this section).

1 quart yogurt	½ cup walnuts,
1 tin (2 ounces) flat	chopped
anchovy fillets	

Drain yogurt through cheesecloth for 3 to 4 hours, stirring occasionally from the bottom to facilitate draining (save the yogurt whey to use in baking, if desired). Mash anchovies and add to yogurt along with walnuts. Serve with crackers.

Makes 1½ to 1¾ cups.

TOFU-SESAME DIP

This dip is really a delightful garlicky hummus. Augmented with other goodies — tomatoes, cucumbers, and lettuce, for instance — it also makes an excellent sandwich filling.

8 ounces tofu	½ teaspoon salt
3 tablespoons lemon or lime juice (usually 1 large lemon or lime)	Pepper to taste
	Chopped Italian parsley, for garnish
1 clove garlic, sliced	Chopped onion, for garnish
4 tablespoons tahini (sesame paste)	

Place first 6 ingredients in a blender or food processor and blend until smooth. To serve, place in a shallow bowl and sprinkle with chopped parsley and onion. Offer wedges of pita to scoop it up.

Makes ample hors d'oeuvre for 4.

CHINESE SOUP WITH TOMATOES

This slightly gingery and attractive soup is Jane's close approximation of one she enjoyed in China while touring with a group of American runners.

1 teaspoon sesame oil	2 large tomatoes, skinned, seeded, and sliced
1 teaspoon chopped fresh ginger root	
6 cups chicken broth	Chopped fresh parsley, for garnish (optional)
2 tablespoons each cornstarch, sherry, and soy sauce	

Heat oil in a large saucepan and sauté ginger briefly. Add broth and simmer for 5 minutes. Mix together cornstarch, sherry, and soy sauce. Stir into soup mixture and simmer until slightly thickened. Remove from heat, add tomatoes, and ladle into bowls. Garnish with parsley if desired.

Serves 6.

JANE'S FOUR-GRAIN CRACKERS

These uniquely flavored crackers are surprisingly easy to make. One short cut is to roll out the dough directly onto the baking sheet.

4 tablespoons each
whole millet, rolled
oats, and rye flour
1¼ cups whole wheat
pastry flour
½ teaspoon each baking
soda, baking powder,
and salt

1 teaspoon whole cumin
seed
3 tablespoons chicken
fat or margarine
½ cup yogurt or
buttermilk
(approximately)

Mix all dry ingredients together. Cut in fat. Mix in only enough yogurt or buttermilk to make the dough stick together. Cover and let rest at least 30 minutes. Roll out dough on a floured surface until to about ⅛-inch thick. Place on a baking sheet. Prick with a fork and score into 2-inch squares with a pastry wheel. Bake at 350°F. for about 15 minutes or until dry and lightly browned. Cool on racks and break apart.   *Yield: 3 dozen 2-inch crackers.*

SPINACH CRÊPES

These rich crêpes make a wonderful luncheon or supper dish.

FILLING:

2 tablespoons butter
¼ pound mushrooms,
sliced
2 tablespoons minced
shallots
10 ounces fresh or
frozen spinach,
chopped
Dash of nutmeg
1 egg
Salt and pepper to taste

1 cup thick yogurt
(drain yogurt through
cheesecloth for about
3 hours, reserving
whey to use in batter
below; somewhat
more than 1 pint of
yogurt is needed to
get 1 cup of thick
yogurt)

In a skillet, melt butter and sauté mushrooms and shallots until soft. Squeeze excess water from frozen spinach — there's no need to cook it. (If using fresh spinach, steam it briefly, covered, on top of the mushrooms and shallots.) Remove from heat and combine with remaining ingredients. Then set aside while preparing the batter (below). *Makes enough filling for 8 crêpes or 4 servings.*

BATTER:

1 cup whey (from draining yogurt, above)	2 eggs 1 cup whole wheat pastry flour

Place all ingredients in a blender, mix until smooth, and let stand for 1 hour. Grease a crêpe pan with no-stick spray. For each crêpe, pour in a spoonful of batter, instantly swirling it around the pan so that it spreads evenly to the edges in a thin film. Cook quickly until golden brown, 1 to 2 minutes, then turn and brown the other side, about another minute. As the crêpes are cooked, pile them on top of one another, keeping them warm under an inverted plate or pot lid (if it's necessary to keep them warm for a good while, store them in a low oven).

Assembly: Divide filling among the crêpes; roll up crêpes and place in a shallow 2-quart casserole dish. Pour Velouté Sauce (below) over top, sprinkle with grated cheese, and bake at 350°F. for about 25 minutes. *Makes about 8 crêpes.*

VELOUTÉ SAUCE

2 tablespoons butter	Salt and pepper to taste
2 tablespoons flour	4 tablespoons grated
1¼ cups well-seasoned chicken stock	cheese

Melt butter. Whisk in flour. Slowly stir in chicken stock and cook until thickened. Add seasonings as desired and use cheese to sprinkle over top of crêpes. *Yield: about 1¾ cups.*

JANE'S BREAD-MAKING TIPS
AND OTHER TECHNIQUES

• For years I believed that kneading bread dough was therapeutic, and it probably is, but if you have a heavy-duty food processor, it can do the job just as well in a matter of seconds. I usually finish kneading by hand.

• Many people err in bread making by adding too much flour, resulting in a dry, hard loaf. Bread dough gets less sticky as you knead it.

• Except in rich holiday breads, sugar and fat are not needed in bread making. Fat helps preserve freshness if you need to keep bread around for several days, but I usually store everything in the freezer and take out just what I need. Usually, homemade bread doesn't last long enough to get stale!

• Most bread recipes call for twice as much salt as is necessary. A bit of salt helps control the action of the yeast and contributes to flavor, but most people use much more than is needed. In fact, I rarely use salt in breads at all anymore.

• Most breads do not require sugar to activate the yeast, as popular myth would have it. A teaspoon of yeast, used in a sponge of water and flour, can make a 3-loaf batch of dough rise beautifully.

• About ¼ teaspoon of ground ginger added to bread

dough gives it an indefinable extra quality and sup-
posedly has a salutary effect on the yeast.

• Most bread can be baked in an oven that is either
cold or preheated, so if you don't have time to preheat,
don't worry about it.

• Save the water from boiling potatoes and other
vegetables and use it in making bread, in soup stock, in
pancake batter, and in other recipes in which it can
replace water.

• Store bananas for up to a month by peeling them,
dipping them in lemon juice, and freezing them in
plastic bags for use in baking and for making milk-
shakes, desserts, and other foods.

• I found I can make my own yogurt without any
fancy equipment. Heat skim milk just to the boiling
point, cool it to 115°F., and mix in 1 tablespoon of
plain yogurt for each quart of milk. Pour the cultured
milk into pint jars, screw on lids, and set the jars in a
large pot filled with hot water. Cover the pot and let it
cool down for 4 or 5 hours, or overnight, and the yogurt
will be done. For those with pilot-light ovens, the jars of
cultured milk may be put on a flat pan and left in the
closed oven for 4 or 5 hours, or until it sets up. Yogurt
keeps longer than fluid milk and is versatile in cooking.
You can use whole milk, reconstituted dry milk, or even
evaporated milk, as well as the skim milk, with good
results.

JANE'S NEW IMPROVED SUPER CHEWY BAGELS

These bagels have a hearty yeast flavor that's enhanced by the potato water. They are delicious with honey and butter as well as with the more traditional cream cheese.

1 teaspoon active dry yeast	4 cups unbleached flour (use part whole wheat or rye if desired)
1½ cups warm water (saved from boiling potatoes or other vegetables)	1 teaspoon salt
	Sesame seeds (optional)

Make a sponge by combining yeast, ½ cup of the warm potato water, and ½ cup flour to make a fairly thick batter that you can still stir. Place the mixture in a warm place and let sit for at least 2 hours until light and bubbly. In a food processor or large bowl, combine the sponge, the remaining 1 cup potato water, salt, and enough of the remaining flour to make a very stiff dough. Knead until smooth and elastic. Place dough in a greased bowl, cover, and let rise until almost double. Punch down, roll dough into a sausage, and cut it into 12 pieces. Roll each piece into a ball and let rest, covered, for about 10 minutes. Form into doughnut shapes by poking your finger through the center of each ball. Place bagels on a greased baking sheet, cover with a dry towel, and let rise for 20 minutes in a warm place. Bring about a gallon of water to a boil in a large, shallow pot and drop about 4 bagels at a time into the water. Boil for about 5 minutes, turning once gently. Remove with a slotted spoon, and place again on baking sheet. Sprinkle with sesame seeds if desired (if the seeds resist sticking, brush bagel tops with a whole-egg wash). Bake at 400°F. for about 20 minutes or until lightly browned. Split, toast, and spread with cream cheese or your favorite topping. Bagels not eaten the first day should be frozen for later use (split bagels before freezing so they'll be ready to eat all the sooner). *Makes 1 dozen.*

BEET PUMPERNICKEL

This bread has an attractive raspberry red crust and good flavor. Because of its dense texture, it does not rise as high as many breads. If you prefer a lighter, more finely grained bread, you might want to substitute unbleached white flour for some or all of the whole wheat.

1 teaspoon active dry yeast	1 tablespoon caraway seeds (optional)
½ cup warm water	2 to 3 cups whole wheat bread flour
½ cup unbleached flour	2 cups rye flour
1½ cups puréed cooked beets	
1 teaspoon salt (optional)	

Make a sponge with yeast, water, and unbleached flour. Let sit, covered, in a warm place for at least 2 hours or until the sponge is light and frothy. Pour into a food processor with the remaining ingredients, reserving 1 cup of whole wheat flour, or mix together by hand in a large bowl. Use enough flour to make a firm dough. Knead well, in processor or by hand. Place dough in a lightly floured bowl, cover with a large plastic bag, and let rise about 1 hour in a warm place. Punch down and shape into 2 round loaves. Place loaves on greased pie plates and let rise another 30 minutes. Slash an "X" on top of each loaf with a razor blade. Place in cold oven and turn heat to 375°F. Bake for about 50 minutes or until loaf sounds hollow when tapped. *Makes 2 loaves.*

ZUCCHINI FRENCH BREAD

For a long while Jane has not used sugar or shortening in her French bread; more recently she has omitted the salt as well. She finds she doesn't miss it.

1 teaspoon active dry yeast	1 to 2 cups puréed zucchini
4 to 6½ cups unbleached flour	1 teaspoon salt (optional)
½ cup water	

Mix yeast, ½ cup of the flour, and water together in a bowl to make a sponge, and set in a warm place for 2 hours or until the sponge is light and frothy. Using a food processor or large bowl, combine sponge with remaining ingredients, incorporating enough flour to make a soft dough. Knead by hand, or process, until smooth and satiny. Cover and let rise until doubled. Form into long loaves and place in greased oblong pans. Let rest for 5 minutes, then slash diagonally with a razor. Place in a cold oven set at 400°F.; bake for about 40 minutes. *Makes 2 loaves.*

GREEN MAYONNAISE

A whole range of flavor possibilities can be achieved by varying the herbs in this recipe, and adding the yogurt both frees up the consistency and gives a welcome tartness.

1 egg yolk	1 teaspoon Dijon mustard
1 cup packed fresh green herbs (basil, oregano, garlic, chives, parsley, and tarragon, or whatever is available)	⅔ cup corn oil, more or less
	½ cup yogurt (optional)
	Pepper to taste
1 tablespoon wine vinegar	

Place egg yolk, herbs, vinegar, mustard, and 2 tablespoons of the oil in a food processor or blender. Mix until smooth. Slowly dribble in more oil as needed to make a smooth mayonnaise. To make the consistency of salad dressing, add yogurt, season with pepper, and mix well. *Makes 1¼ cups.*

BLUEBERRY TART

Another delectable, and really quite easy, way to use up some of the summer's blueberries. Especially good served with ice cream.

CRUST:
Use your favorite recipe, or try this whole wheat crust.

¼ cup butter or margarine, melted	1 tablespoon maple syrup (optional)
2 tablespoons chicken fat, melted	1¼ cups whole wheat pastry flour

Heat butter and chicken fat until foamy; remove from heat. Add syrup if desired. Mix in flour to make pastry dough. Press into a straight-sided 9-inch tart pan or a pie plate.

FILLING:

4 cups blueberries, reserving about 1 cup for topping	4 to 6 tablespoons maple syrup
3 tablespoons whole wheat pastry flour	Cinnamon (optional)

Place blueberries in pie crust. Sift flour over berries and drizzle with syrup; dust with cinnamon if desired. Bake at 350°F. for about 50 minutes, until berries are thickened and crust is nicely browned. Remove from oven and immediately pour reserved fresh blueberries over the top. Serve while still warm. *Makes one 9-inch tart.*

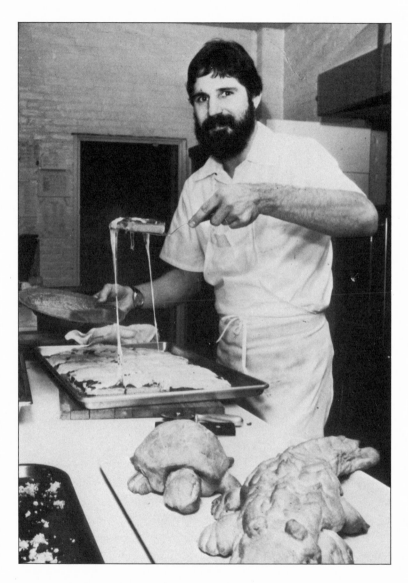

Timmy Sheyda serving his "natural" pizza.

School Lunches Like Never Before!

TIMMY SHEYDA
Waterbury Elementary School
Waterbury, Vermont

What other New England chefs, like Jane Nordstrom in the previous segment, are doing for their families, Timmy Sheyda is doing for the school-children of Waterbury, Vermont — working hard and creatively to offer highly nutritious and inviting meals.

Timmy, who graduated from Dartmouth College in 1972, at first followed a more traditional food service career. He began his career working in the college kitchen, then continued as a chef in some of the area's more prestigious restaurants. But two things happened: he tired of always working nights and weekends when he wanted to be with his young family, and he became interested in simpler, more healthful food. "I'm not a fanatic," he says, "just trying to eat healthily."

The children of the Waterbury Elementary School are the fortunate beneficiaries of Timmy's new direction. When they are grown, their school lunch memories won't include mystery meat loaf, gluey mashed potatoes, and pallid peas. Instead, they'll remember hearty squares of homemade pizza, fresh, hot muffins and breads, Carobanas (frozen bananas dipped in carob syrup and gorp), and an 18-foot salad bar loaded with enough choices to please even the most finicky of the school's 300 daily lunchtime guests (70 percent of the students now take part in the hot-lunch program — a percentage steadily going up).

And Timmy doesn't stop with offering nutritious and exciting lunchtime meals: he also works hard at teaching the students

161

the rules of good nutrition. He runs poster contests, the results of which are posted on the cafeteria walls; he visits the classrooms, taking examples of his message along for all to share; and he invites the students into his kitchen to work with him on his recipes (a good way to practice fractions) or to develop their own.

But it isn't always easy. The budget is a constraint. Both the federal and state governments, upon which Timmy depends for help, have strict, and not always up-to-date, guidelines upon which their help hinges. The federal government, for example, urges low fat, sugar, and salt diets, yet supplies many surplus foods loaded with these unwanted elements. Then, too, yogurt is not yet permitted as a milk substitute, nor is tofu yet an acceptable protein — all of which make Timmy's job even more difficult. Timmy does, however, make extensive use of much of the surplus food — the cheese, whole wheat flour, oats, chicken, peanut butter, and other items — and he rounds out his menu with fresh vegetables and fruits in season, and other foods as needed. To help further, Timmy fills the saltcellars with low-sodium substitutes and refuses to serve chocolate, using carob instead.

Somehow it all works. His lunch program has won wide approval and is now being urged as a model for other schools. Youngsters surveying the daily salad bar (groaning with peanut butter, macaroni and tuna salads, fresh tomato slices, mixed cheeses, garbanzo and kidney beans, coleslaw, sprouts, raw carrots, raisin and pineapple chunk salad, sliced pears, and fresh-fruit gelatin) can be heard to say, "This is the neatest thing we ever had." And at night, their parents often call Timmy at home for that day's favorite recipe.

You are lucky: you don't have to call. Timmy has scaled down several of his top-of-the-chart recipes for all of us to try.

TIMMY SHEYDA'S PIZZA

This is the pizza that the Waterbury Elementary School youngsters are so fond of. It's not only nutritious, it's delicious, and easy to make. The sauce recipe makes more than enough for the two pizzas, so you'll have extra for other dishes as well — a nice bonus!

CRUST:

1 tablespoon active dry yeast
1 cup water (about 115° F.)
⅓ cup oil
2 tablespoons honey
3 cups whole wheat flour, or more as needed
1 teaspoon salt
2 tablespoons noninstant milk powder

1 tablespoon brewer's yeast flakes (also called nutritional yeast)
12 ounces grated mozzarella cheese or crumbled tofu (or both)

Stir together yeast, water, oil, and honey. Let yeast soften while you measure out remaining ingredients, then combine all ingredients and knead for 10 to 15 minutes ("I throw my dough into the food processor and let *it* knead the dough while I get the sauce together"). Add more flour if needed. Place dough in an oiled bowl, cover, and let rise in a warm place until doubled. Punch down, divide in half, and roll each half onto an oiled pizza pan (12 to 14 inches in diameter). Let rise about 15 minutes. Bake for 10 minutes at 350°F., until crust just starts to turn brown. Remove from oven and brush with oil. When you're ready to make your pizza, spread 1 cup of sauce (below) on each crust, then top generously with grated mozzarella or crumbled tofu, or both. Bake in a 400° oven for 5 to 10 minutes, until cheese is bubbling. Serve immediately.   *Makes 2 good-sized pizzas, 8 slices each.*

Recipe continues on next page

TIM SHEYDA'S PIZZA continued

SAUCE:

1 medium onion, diced
1 stalk celery, diced
1 small green pepper, diced
1 clove garlic, crushed
Oil, for sautéing
2 teaspoons dried basil leaves

1 teaspoon dried oregano leaves
Dash of cayenne
1 can (28 ounces) crushed tomatoes

Sauté onion, celery, pepper, and garlic in a small amount of oil. Add remaining ingredients and simmer until thick. When crust is ready, spread approximately 1 cup sauce on each pizza and bake as directed above. Since the recipe makes about 3½ cups sauce, you can use the rest to make Spanish omelets the next morning, or another favorite dish. The sauce can also be frozen for future use. (Timmy freezes his extra sauce in ice cube trays, then pops the cubes into a freezer storage bag. When needed, he takes as many as he wants out of the freezer; the cubes thaw quickly.)

Makes more than enough sauce for 2 good-sized pizzas.

POPCORN BALLS

Timmy flavors his popcorn balls with barley malt. Barley malt (available in most health food stores) is a more complex sugar than refined sugar and contains B vitamins and many essential minerals. The popcorn balls made this way are softer, not too sweet, and have a molasseslike flavor. When planning for a crowd, figure that ½ cup popping corn will make about six cups of popped corn.

2 tablespoons oil
½ cup popping corn
¼ cup butter

½ cup liquid barley malt

Pop the corn in the heated oil and set aside. Heat the butter in a large saucepan, add the barley malt, and stir. Boil for 1 minute. Add the popped corn and stir it until evenly coated. Remove from heat. As soon as corn is cool enough to handle, shape into balls by squeezing between both hands. (Dip hands in water frequently to keep corn from sticking.)

Makes about 18 tennis-ball-sized balls — assuming not too much is eaten in process.

SWEET POTATO AND BANANA BREAD

Timmy uses this delicious, and moist, bread to add still another vegetable element to his school lunch menu. But it also makes a tasty snack spread with cream cheese or low-fat cottage cheese.

2 cups whole wheat
  flour (pastry flour
  preferred)
1 teaspoon salt
1 teaspoon baking
  powder (preferably
  aluminum-free,
  available at health
  food stores)
2 teaspoons baking soda
½ teaspoon nutmeg
½ teaspoon cinnamon
¼ teaspoon ground
  cloves

¼ teaspoon ginger
½ cup honey
1 large cooked sweet
  potato, mashed
2 eggs, beaten
½ cup oil
2 very ripe bananas,
  mashed
½ cup chopped nuts
½ cup raisins, plumped
  in ½ cup orange juice

Combine all dry ingredients in a large bowl. Mix together remaining ingredients and stir into dry mixture, stirring just enough to avoid lumps. Pour into an oiled and floured 9- by 9-inch pan. Bake for 45 minutes at 350°F., or until a toothpick inserted in the center comes out clean. *Makes 9 to 12 pieces.*

TIMMY SHEYDA ON USING CAROB

Carob flour is the ground-up dried fruit of the carob tree. It is a delicious food in its own right but has also become a popular substitute for chocolate and cocoa. Carob is virtually fat-free, while baking chocolate is half fat; carob, naturally sweet, has only about one-third the calories of baking chocolate and half the calories of cocoa. Carob does not interrupt the body's assimilation of calcium (as does the oxalic acid in chocolate); carob also contains only a tiny fraction of the stimulants caffeine and theobromine that are found in chocolate. While carob does not taste like chocolate, it makes a good and far more healthful substitute.

Here are some guides for cooking with carob.

1. As a substitute for cocoa, use equal amounts of carob powder.

2. As a substitute for *melted semisweet chocolate,* use the Carob Syrup recipe (following), but add 2 tablespoons butter.

3. As a substitute for *melted bitter chocolate,* use the Carob Syrup recipe, but omit the sweetener. Use ¼ cup syrup for every 2 squares bitter chocolate.

CAROBANAS

These are a popular dessert at the Waterbury Elementary School. They also make a very filling and satisfying snack. This is a recipe for four bananas; obviously, Timmy needs many more.

Take 1 bunch of 4 ripe bananas. Peel and cut into 2- to 3-inch lengths. Place on waxed paper and freeze. Prepare Carob Syrup (below) and let it cool. Dip the frozen bananas into the cooled syrup, then roll in chopped walnuts, coconut, Grape-nuts, granola, or any combination. Serve immediately or store in the freezer.

Makes 8 to 12 pieces.

CAROB SYRUP

This recipe will make enough syrup to coat approximately four large bananas cut in two- to three-inch pieces. In addition to using the syrup as a dip for fruit, Timmy uses it as a substitute for chocolate (see his guidelines on using carob just preceding).

1 cup carob powder	¼ cup honey or barley
1 cup water	malt

Combine and bring to a boil in a 1½- or 2-quart saucepan. Simmer, stirring, for several minutes. Cool. *Makes 1½ cups syrup.*

CAROB BROWNIES

Good, moist — and a new taste sensation. Well worth a try!

½ cup oil	¾ cup wheat germ
¾ cup barley malt	¾ cup whole wheat
2 eggs	flour (pastry flour
½ cup carob powder	preferred)
1 tablespoon vanilla	1 tablespoon aluminum-
1 ripe banana, mashed	free baking powder
½ cup plumped raisins	
½ cup chopped nuts,	
plus extra for topping	

Beat together oil, barley malt, eggs, carob powder, vanilla, banana, raisins, and nuts. Separately mix wheat germ, flour, and baking powder. Add flour mixture to egg mixture and stir minimally — do not overbeat. Spread into a 9- by 13-inch oiled and floured pan. Sprinkle a few more chopped nuts on top. Bake for 20 to 25 minutes at 350°F. Let cool before cutting. *Makes 24.*

Paul Heroux with his culinary art.

Culinary Art From Down East

PAUL HEROUX
New Gloucester, Maine

In recent years, much New England cookery has taken on a more sophisticated sheen, and many of its menus have expanded to include some of the world's most cosmopolitan food. This is the cooking you would find practiced in the kitchen of Paul Heroux's woodsy home at the far end of a New Gloucester blacktop.

Paul's cuisine is a subtle blend of the haute cuisine he encountered as a student at the School of the Boston Museum of Fine Arts, the cooking he knew as a boy in New Hampshire, and the culinary experience he gained from his more recent days as chef at No Tomatoes, one of Maine's first "alternative culture" restaurants — all combined with the color and art that dominates Paul's life.

Paul took much of what he had learned at Boston's Le Bocage (classic French techniques such as how to make stocks and sauces, how to prepare vegetables, and how to sharpen knifes), from Cambridge's fine Window Shop bakery (the importance of quality ingredients), and from No Tomatoes (how to achieve a more innovative cuisine) to build a successful catering business in Maine.

But this was not all: at the same time Paul continued his painting and creative clay work. So, while Paul built his business, he also began to show and sell his ceramic pieces. Eventually, his love of pottery crept ahead of his obsession with cooking, and today, Paul has traded his life as a professional cook for a life as a professional art instructor at nearby Bates College and for time to pursue his own artwork. These days, although he still studies to perfect his "culinary arts from Down East," it's only, as Paul puts it, "for the joy of it."

169

ESCABÈCHE
Marinated Shark with Basil and Raspberry Vinegar

Escabèche — *a seldom seen southern European classic* — *combines fried and marinated shark with basil and raspberry vinegar. It makes an excellent supper dish or a conversation-provoking hors d'oeuvre. For the vinegar, you may use the Sweet Raspberry Vinegar given below or one of the raspberry vinegars available at gourmet and specialties shops.*

2½ pounds boneless shark (or swordfish or monkfish), cut into very thin steaks (approximately ¼-inch thick)	½ teaspoon salt
	¼ teaspoon pepper
	Bland oil, for frying
	4 or 5 very ripe tomatoes
½ cup flour	½ cup fresh basil, separated into leaves and tender top sprigs, for garnish
½ cup whole yellow mustard seed	

MARINADE:

⅓ cup raspberry vinegar (use recipe below or own choice)	1 teaspoon fresh thyme (or ½ teaspoon dried)
	2 cloves
½ cup water	½ cup chopped fresh basil
1 onion, sliced	½ cup olive oil
1 bay leaf	

First, prepare the marinade. Combine all ingredients except olive oil in a heavy, noncorrodible saucepan, and simmer gently for 30 minutes. Strain, pressing on the solids to get all possible liquid. Measure, and if necessary add water to make ¾ cup. Combine with olive oil and set aside.

Lay out shark in a single layer on freezer paper or other heavy paper. Combine flour, mustard seed, salt, and pepper, and distribute half of the mixture evenly over fish. Then, with a wooden mallet, pound it in. Turn fish and repeat with the remaining mixture. Next, heat a half-inch layer of oil in a wide, heavy skillet and fry the fish over fairly high heat until it is completely cooked and the mustard seeds are toasted and brown. Turn once with tongs, taking care not to pierce the fish. As each slice browns, transfer to absorbent paper to drain.

Put the fish in a deep serving platter and cover with the marinade. Cover with plastic wrap and let marinate at room temperature for about 2 hours. Baste frequently. At serving time, cut tomatoes into thin slices and layer them with the fish. Garnish generously with the remaining basil and serve at once. This *escabèche* can be prepared a day in advance and held in the refrigerator: just don't add the tomatoes until serving time, and be sure to bring the dish back to room temperature for maximum flavor before serving. *Serves 8.*

SWEET RASPBERRY OR BLACKBERRY VINEGAR

It is important to use the highly acid wine vinegar for this sweet berry vinegar because it becomes so diluted by the berry juice. Without enough acidity, the end product could spoil; don't be tempted to use ordinary white vinegar. The high-acid vinegar is available in specialty and gourmet food stores.

1½ pounds raspberries or blackberries (3 pints)	1 quart European-style red wine vinegar (7% acidity)
½ cup sugar	

Combine berries with sugar and place in jars. Fill with vinegar, apply lids, and process for 10 minutes in a boiling-water bath. Let sealed jars cool, then refrigerate for 3 weeks; then strain and bottle. Use on fruit, in salads, in marinades, and as a sauce component, especially for chicken and duck livers. It's also nice, with sugar, as a light dressing for fresh strawberries. *Makes about 1½ quarts.*

SEAFOOD AND CARROT TART

This tart has a delicately piquant flavor and makes a delightful luncheon or supper dish. Cut into slenderer slices, it can also serve as an appetizer.

1 batch Butter/Lard
Pastry (see recipe
following)
½ cup chopped onion
2 tablespoons butter
1 cup cooked seafood:
crab, shrimp, lobster,
salmon, or any
combination, diced
small
1½ cups finely shredded
sweet orange carrots
1 cup shredded Swiss
cheese
1 small fresh hot
pepper, finely minced

½ teaspoon freshly
crushed coriander
seeds
½ teaspoon minced
fresh thyme or ¼
teaspoon crushed
dried thyme
1 teaspoon
Worcestershire sauce
2 whole eggs plus 2 egg
yolks
⅔ cup medium cream
Salt and pepper to taste

To prepare the shell: Allow chilled Butter/Lard Pastry to come to cool room temperature, then roll it out thin, and fit it into a shallow 10-inch tart form. Prick well all over and freeze. Bake unfilled frozen shell in a preheated 400°F. oven for 20 minutes or until lightly browned.

To prepare the filling and complete: In a medium-sized skillet, sauté the onion in the butter until it is golden. Add seafood and carrots, and permit to cool. Stir in cheese, hot pepper, coriander, thyme, and Worcestershire sauce. Beat eggs and yolks together gently, only enough to mix (try to avoid incorporating too much air), then beat in cream. Combine with seafood mixture, season with salt and pepper, and turn into the partially baked shell. Bake in a preheated 350°F. oven for 30 minutes or until filling is set and crust has finished browning. Serve warm.   *Makes 10 modest slices.*

BUTTER/LARD PASTRY

This nicely textured pastry has excellent flavor and is easy to prepare.

2 cups unbleached flour
Pinch of salt
1 stick (½ cup) unsalted
  butter
¼ cup lard
3 tablespoons ice water,
  more or less as
  needed

Mix flour with salt. Cut in butter and lard until lumps are pea-sized, then flake the mixture through your fingers for a few minutes until fat is well mixed with flour. Dribble in water, tossing and pressing gently, until a stiff dough is formed. (Use as little water as possible.) Press dough into a flattish ball, wrap tightly in plastic, and chill at least 1 hour before using.

Makes ample pastry for one 10-inch tart shell.

CORN SALAD

2 bell peppers, 1 red
  and 1 green, cored
⅓ cup plus 2
  tablespoons corn oil
4 large ears corn,
  cooked
2 cups small red new
  potatoes, cooked
3 tablespoons finely
  chopped red onion
2 teaspoons minced
  fresh tarragon
2 tablespoons minced
  fresh parsley
2 teaspoons Dijon-style
  mustard
1 teaspoon soy sauce
1 tablespoon tarragon
  vinegar
Salt and pepper to taste

Cut peppers into thin strips; then, in a medium-sized skillet, sauté over high heat in 2 tablespoons of the oil until peppers are browned in spots. Set aside. Cut corn from the cob and dice potatoes fairly small. Mix remaining ⅓ cup of oil with onion, herbs, mustard, soy sauce, and vinegar. Stir in the peppers, then add the remaining vegetables and season to taste. Stir well and chill in a tightly covered 2-quart bowl for at least 2 hours, so flavors have a chance to blend. This salad will keep well in the refrigerator for 2 or 3 days. *Makes 6 to 8 generous servings.*

SOUR FRENCH BREAD

This sour dough makes bread with an excellent punchy flavor and a good bitey crust.

2 cups low-fat yogurt
2 tablespoons sugar
1 tablespoon salt
1½ cups boiling water
2 tablespoons (2
    envelopes) active dry
    yeast
7 to 8 cups unbleached
    bread flour
    (approximately)

Cornmeal for pans
4 baguette pans (long,
    narrow pans for
    French bread)
Glaze: 1 egg white,
    beaten with 1
    tablespoon water

Combine yogurt, sugar, and salt in a large heatproof bowl. Pour in the boiling water and stir well. When mixture is tepid, sprinkle on the yeast and allow the mixture to sit for 10 minutes, or until the yeast is completely dissolved. Beat well, then start stirring in the flour. Continue to add flour until dough is very stiff, then turn out onto a floured board and knead, adding more flour as necessary, until you have a smooth, shiny dough that is not sticky. Return to bowl, cover loosely with a barely damp tea towel, and permit to rise until fully doubled. Dough may be formed into loaves at this point, but the flavor will be improved if dough is punched down and permitted to rise again at least once, ideally twice, before shaping and baking. (Each successive rising will take less time.)

Punch down dough and shape into 4 long loaves. Place each in a cornmeal-sprinkled pan and allow to rise, uncovered. Preheat oven to 400°F. Slash risen loaves with a razor blade and place them in oven. Bake 15 minutes, lower heat to 350°, and bake 40 minutes longer or until loaves are nicely browned and sound hollow when tapped. About 5 minutes before you expect them to be done, brush loaves with glaze. When done, turn out of pans immediately and cool on wire racks. *Makes 4 loaves.*

LEMON MOUSSE
(From Le Bocage)

This rich mousse from Boston's Le Bocage restaurant is very tart and oh, so good!

1 package (1 tablespoon) unflavored gelatin	Juice of 3 lemons
	3 eggs, separated
Zest of 2 lemons, grated fine	½ cup plus 3 tablespoons sugar
	1½ cups heavy cream

Combine gelatin, zest, and juice in a noncorrodible saucepan and heat, stirring, just until gelatin is thoroughly dissolved. Beat egg yolks with ½ cup sugar until the mixture is thick and pale, then stir in the slightly cooled gelatin mixture. Chill until thick and almost, but not quite, set. Beat egg whites with the remaining 3 tablespoons sugar until they form stiff but still shiny peaks, then whip the cream and fold everything together. Spoon into stemmed glasses or other decorative serving bowls and chill until set.

Makes 10 small servings.

Bill Sammons finishes up his rack of lamb.

Haute Cuisine High Over The South End

BILL SAMMONS
Boston, Massachusetts

Perhaps it's chiefly for the "relaxation and immediate gratification," as he puts it, that Bill Sammons, prominent Boston-area pediatrician, retreats so happily to his fourth floor, city-view kitchen to do so much of the cooking — simple cuisine for the week nights, fancier gourmet fare for weekends.

Bill Sammon's interest in cooking began in his mother's kitchen, where she encouraged him to experiment "to see what would happen." There, he did little measuring, a habit which persists, and which, he adds smiling, may account for his "probably 25 percent error factor" (evidence of which we have not found).

Even while at medical school, Bill found time to develop his interest in good food and wine, but it wasn't until he made Boston his home and began courses in French and northern Italian cooking at the Boston Center for Adult Education that this interest fully blossomed. Bill credits these courses and the chef at the South Londonderry, Vermont, Three Clock Inn (a frequent vacation spot) — plus his almost weekly pot of home-simmered veal stock — for whatever culinary kudos he may deserve.

However, Bill also firmly believes in the importance of careful and creative food shopping, and whenever possible, the use of fresh produce — a belief he puts into action whenever he can from his rooftop salad garden. But, whether you select your summer greens from your garden or from your local grocer, the following recipes from Bill Sammons are sure pleasers.

CARROT SOUP

Bill Sammons purées this creamy and lightly flavored soup using a conical strainer and a wooden spoon, but we found that a blender or a food processor also gives a lovely, smooth texture.

2 large onions, chopped
4 tablespoons unsalted
   butter
1 pound carrots,
   shredded
4 to 6 cups chicken
   stock
½ cup uncooked rice
4 shallots, minced
Salt and pepper to taste

1 to 2 teaspoons dried
   chervil (more fresh, if
   available)
⅓ cup fresh orange juice
1 cup heavy cream
½ cup sour cream, plus
   extra for topping
Nutmeg or paprika, for
   garnish

In a good-sized stockpot, sauté onions in butter until translucent; add shredded carrots and stir over medium heat until wilted (4 to 5 minutes). Add chicken stock and bring to a boil. Add rice, shallots, salt, pepper, and chervil. Simmer for 40 minutes. Purée. Return to pot and bring back to boil. Then remove from heat and add orange juice, heavy cream, and sour cream. Heat thoroughly and serve immediately, dusted with nutmeg or paprika. The soup may be served in individual bowls or cups, each with its own dollop of sour cream. *Makes 8 to 9 cups.*

WATERCRESS SOUP

Accompanied with hefty slices of home-baked rye or wheat bread, this tangy, substantial soup could be used to good advantage as a main dish.

4 large leeks or 4
  medium onions,
  thinly sliced
4 tablespoons butter
6 large potatoes
4 to 6 cups chicken
  stock (amount
  depends on
  consistency desired)
2 cups chopped
  watercress

2 cups heavy cream
Salt and pepper to taste
  (optional)
Grated nutmeg, for
  garnish
½ cup sour cream, for
  topping
½ to 1 teaspoon
  horseradish (optional)

In a good-sized stockpot, sauté sliced leeks or onions in butter until just softened. Peel and dice potatoes and add to onions along with the stock. Bring mixture to a boil and simmer until potatoes are cooked. Add the watercress, reserving a small amount for garnish, and simmer for another 3 to 4 minutes. Purée; then return mixture to pot and reheat. Add cream but do not boil; a dash of salt and pepper may be added if desired. Serve sprinkled with the reserved watercress and grated nutmeg and topped with dollops of the sour cream. If the soup isn't as tangy as desired, add horseradish.

Makes 8 generous servings.

STARBUCK'S RED PEPPER SOUP

This individualistic, but easy-to-prepare, soup may not be for everyone. However, for those who enjoy new tastes, here's a winner.

4 to 6 large red sweet peppers, cleaned and julienned	Port or Madeira wine to taste
4 tablespoons butter	2 egg yolks
4 cups beef broth (bouillon is usually too salty)	½ to 1 cup heavy cream
	Thyme or cayenne pepper to taste

In a soup pot, sauté peppers briefly in butter to soften lightly, retaining a few pieces for garnish. Add beef broth and simmer until peppers are quite soft. Remove peppers and purée with a little broth; return to pot and reheat. Add wine to taste. Mix egg yolks with about 4 tablespoons cream; add a little hot soup and whisk, then whisk the mixture back into the soup. Add enough of the remaining cream to reach the desired consistency. Season lightly with thyme or cayenne pepper. *Serves 8.*

RACK OR CROWN ROAST OF LAMB

Presenting lamb in this elegant fashion is a sure crowd pleaser. Keep in mind that the size of the roast will affect its roasting time, and be sure to have the meat at room temperature when you begin.

1 rack or crown of lamb (3 to 5 pounds)	2 cloves garlic, minced
Olive oil, to cover lamb	¼ cup minced fresh parsley
Dijon mustard, to brush on lamb	¼ teaspoon rosemary, crushed
1 cup fresh bread crumbs, or ground almonds or macadamia nuts	½ teaspoon pepper
	¼ teaspoon thyme

Brush meat with olive oil and roast at 400°F. for 20 minutes. Brush on mustard. Mix crumbs or ground nuts with garlic, parsley, rosemary, pepper, and thyme, and gently apply a coating over the mustard by hand. Return to oven and continue to roast at 375°F. for 25 to 35 minutes (lamb should be pink inside after about 25 minutes of cooking). Serve with a mustard or garlic hollandaise sauce, if desired. *Serves 6 to 8.*

SHRIMP CURRY

This delicious curry is so good it's almost sinful. However, the successful use of curry powder and cayenne depends on its original strength (and age). For those not too familiar with curry, a good rule of thumb might be 2 to 2½ teaspoons curry and ⅛ to ¼ teaspoon each cayenne and ginger per pint of cream.

Bouillon or salted water	Heavy cream, 1 cup for
4 to 6 large shrimps per	every 2 people
person	Curry powder to taste
1 stalk celery, diced	Cayenne pepper to taste
2 shallots, minced	Ginger to taste
3 tablespoons butter	Lemon juice (optional)

In a large kettle, bring ample bouillon or salted water to a boil. Add the shrimp, shells on, and cook until they are just pink — not completely cooked (rarely more than a minute). Drain well; shell and devein, and set aside. Sauté the celery and shallots in butter until soft. Add the cream and reduce over high heat (it will not burn) until nearly the desired thickness (about 10 minutes). Remove from heat and strain. Add curry, cayenne, and ginger to the strained sauce to taste. Add shrimp and reheat, reducing sauce to desired consistency. Adjust taste with a few drops of lemon juice, if desired, and serve immediately. A lovely, light rice makes the ideal bed for this curry. *Recipe serves 1 generously; multiply as wanted.*

RICE PILAF WITH RAISINS AND HAZELNUTS

The use of an herbed wine for plumping the raisins gives this pilaf an intriguing, distinctive taste.

1 cup rice (wild rice is best, if available)	¼ cup raisins, plumped in port wine, lightly
⅓ cup butter	seasoned with
2 cups beef broth	turmeric, to cover
¼ cup coarsely chopped hazelnuts	

In a medium-sized ovenproof saucepan, sauté rice in butter until translucent. Add broth and bring to boil. Cover pot with 2 paper towels and cover tightly with lid. Bake at 375°F. for 20 minutes. Remove lid and toweling, and fluff rice with fork. Add nuts and raisins, and any remaining port if desired. This pilaf can be kept warm over hot water until ready to serve.   *Serves 4 to 6.*

ASPARAGUS WITH ORANGE SAUCE

A nice change of pace for asparagus in season. The sauce can be kept warm over hot water while the asparagus cooks.

2 tablespoons water	Pinch of pepper
2 teaspoons lemon juice	3 egg yolks
6 tablespoons orange or tangerine juice	6 tablespoons unsalted butter, melted
2 teaspoons finely grated orange or tangerine rind	1 to 2 pounds fresh asparagus (amount depends on guests' asparagus appetite)
½ teaspoon salt	

To make the sauce, combine water, lemon juice, 4 tablespoons of the fruit juice, the fruit rind, salt, and pepper in a saucepan. Reduce over moderate heat to 3 or 4 tablespoons. Add the egg yolks one at a time, whisking over low heat until very thick. Remove from heat and slowly dribble in butter, whisking constantly. Slowly add the remaining fruit juice, a teaspoon at a time. Strain if you wish (Bill Sammons prefers the rind left in). If necessary, keep sauce warm over a pan of warm water while asparagus cooks. Remove tough ends of asparagus and cook tips only 4 to 7 minutes, until bright green but still slightly crisp. When asparagus is ready, place sauce in a warmed ceramic bowl and serve with the asparagus.

Enough for 4 to 6.

REFRIGERATOR CHEESE PIE

This recipe makes ample filling for a 10-inch pie, with extra to spare. If you prefer a less lemony pie, you might want to use smaller lemons.

2 cups crumbs from
    cinnamon graham
    crackers or cinnamon
    zwieback
3 tablespoons butter,
    melted
1 envelope (1
    tablespoon)
    unflavored gelatin

1¼ cups cold milk
2 eggs, separated
¼ teaspoon salt
⅔ cup sugar
Rind of 2 lemons,
    grated
Juice of 2 large lemons
1½ cups cottage cheese
½ cup whipping cream

Combine crumbs and melted butter to make a crust, and pat into pie plate. Soften gelatin in ¼ cup of the milk (to soften gelatin in milk, sprinkle in and allow to sit, unstirred, for about 20 minutes). Blend 2 egg yolks in top of a double boiler; add salt, sugar, and the remaining cup of milk. Cook over hot water, stirring constantly, until mixture coats a silver spoon (do not allow water to reach a boil). Stir the gelatin mixture in the custard until thoroughly dissolved. Chill in refrigerator until mixture starts to thicken and is a mayonnaiselike consistency. Put lemon rind, lemon juice, and cottage cheese in a blender and blend until smooth. Whip the egg whites, then the whipping cream. Fold the cheese mixture, then the whipped cream, and then the beaten egg whites into the chilled custard. Pour into prepared crust and refrigerate until ready to serve. *Serves 8 to 10.*

SHERRY CREAM PIE

A lovely, light pie reminiscent, in one taster's opinion, of Bailey's Irish Cream. Any extra filling can be spooned into dessert glasses and served as a special pudding.

1½ cups crushed
chocolate wafers
4 tablespoons butter,
melted
1 envelope unflavored
gelatin
1¼ cups cold milk
3 eggs, separated

½ cup sugar
Pinch of salt
¼ teaspoon nutmeg
½ cup sherry wine
1 cup whipping cream
Additional chocolate
crumbs or grated
chocolate, for garnish

Mix crushed wafers (a good trick for crushing wafers is to put them in a plastic bag first) with melted butter and pat into large (9- or 10-inch) pie plate. Refrigerate. Soften gelatin in ¼ cup of the milk (to soften, sprinkle lightly over milk and set aside, unstirred, for about 20 minutes). Put egg yolks in top of a double boiler, beat slightly, then add sugar and the remaining cup of milk. Cook over hot water about 10 minutes (watching that the water does not come to a full boil), until mixture coats a silver spoon. Remove from heat. Add the gelatin mixture, salt, and nutmeg, and stir until gelatin is completely dissolved. Add the sherry very slowly, stirring constantly (mixture will curdle if sherry is added too quickly). Refrigerate until gelatin mixture begins to thicken (this takes about 30 to 45 minutes). Beat egg whites, whip cream separately, then gently fold both into pie filling. Pour into the prepared pie shell and sprinkle with extra chocolate crumbs or grated chocolate. Refrigerate until ready to serve. *Serves 8 to 10.*

Leslie Land between steps.

From Chez Panisse to Simpler Things

LESLIE LAND
Cushing, Maine

Leslie Land's exposure to haute cuisine began early: her parents introduced her to fine French cookery as a youngster. Her interest was further piqued at the trendy eateries of the San Francisco Bay area during her college days at Berkeley and then fine-tuned by a job as one of the first chefs at Chez Panisse. And for some time, her cooking, as both chef and caterer, reflected this more elaborate cuisine.

However, now in Maine, Leslie finds that, though her "interest in food is greater than it's ever been" it is less prescribed. Still an accomplished cook, as her recipes here attest, Leslie notes that her cooking is evolving toward simpler things, toward using what's available and having the patience to wait until things are fresh again. Today she is more interested in getting down to the essences of food — what she calls "its anthropology."

This has led her away from her life as a caterer of fancy platters, chocolate-filled cream-puff swans, and spun-sugar filigree, to working in her two gardens and putting up much of their produce, to working with organizations concerned with food-related policy, and especially, to writing "Good Food," a syndicated column now read on both seacoasts and many places between. In a recent column, Leslie urged her readers, "Don't be intimidated by recipe worship! Once you know the basics, you can do anything!"

This is only one of her newfound feelings about cooking that Leslie hopes to share with her readers — both through her column and through a new cookbook she is now preparing.

SHELLFISH PLATTER WITH MAYONNAISE

This elegant platter is seafood with a splash. Not only is it delicious, it's also a real eye-catcher as an hors d'oeuvre or a buffet supper dish. Leslie arranges it on a bed of rockweed or other natural bedding and serves it with her own mayonnaise or an aioli. You can use either of these or your own favorite seafood dressing. But remember, when planning to use this dish, it does take time.

COURT BOUILLON:

Equal parts water and white wine (enough to cover the shrimp generously)
1 lemon, quartered

1 bay leaf
2 sprigs each parsley and celery greens
8 or 10 peppercorns
5 or 6 coriander seeds

SHELLFISH:

1 pound North Atlantic shrimp (weighed in the shell)
½ pound scallops

½ pound picked crabmeat
2 lobsters

Combine bouillon ingredients and cook at a full boil for about 5 minutes. Dump the shrimp into the boiling liquid and cook for no more than 2 minutes. Drain, reserving broth. Shell the shrimp and put aside, returning shells and seasonings to the broth. (Use shells only if shrimp are very fresh.) Cook the broth about 45 minutes, uncovered, then strain. Put enough of the broth in a heavy, nonaluminum pan to barely cover the scallops. Bring the mixture to a gentle simmer, add the scallops, and cook for 5 minutes, until they are barely opaque. Drain scallops and put aside; and return cooking liquid to large pot of broth. Scrub the crabs and lobsters and steam them over 2 inches of boiling water for about 20 minutes. Pick out meat and put aside; save the boiling water and add it and the lobster shells to the shrimp broth. Chill the prepared shellfish until needed. Reduce the broth to half its volume, strain, and freeze for future use in making chowders or sauces that call for fish stock. Serve shellfish with a homemade mayonnaise or aioli (recipes follow). *Serves 8 as a supper dish, more as an hors d'oeuvre.*

LESLIE'S MAYONNAISE

Homemade mayonnaise is so much better — if you don't make your own, do try Leslie's. And do note her tip on how to deal with mayonnaise that may have separated.

4 egg yolks, at room temperature	1 cup olive oil
½ teaspoon salt	1 cup peanut oil, or less as needed
½ teaspoon dry mustard	2 teaspoons very hot water
½ teaspoon sugar	
3 to 4 tablespoons lemon juice as needed	

Place a heavy bowl on a folded damp towel (to prevent slipping) and put in the egg yolks. Season with salt, mustard, and sugar; add 1½ teaspoons lemon juice. Begin stirring the mixture with a whisk. When the ingredients are well blended, start dripping in the olive oil, a little at a time. Stop adding oil occasionally to be sure the yolks are absorbing it, but don't stop stirring. If/when olive oil is absorbed, switch to the peanut oil. After a cup or so of oil is added, the sauce will be almost too thick to stir. Mix in 1 tablespoon of lemon juice (or more if needed) and keep going until mayonnaise is at the desired consistency. Beat in 2 teaspoons of very hot water at the end to lighten and bind the sauce. Add more sugar, salt, or lemon juice to taste. Store tightly covered in the refrigerator; it will keep for about 10 days. Do not stir while cold, or it will separate. If the mayonnaise separates, place either 4 teaspoons of prepared mustard or 1 egg yolk in a bowl and slowly drip in the separated mixture, stirring constantly. *Makes 2½ to 3 cups.*

AIOLI

Aioli makes an excellent dressing for vegetables as well as seafood. Leslie reminds us that most vegetables for dipping should be blanched briefly and then chilled. That way they are absorbent as well as crisp.

6 to 8 cloves garlic	Dash of white pepper
1 teaspoon salt	2 teaspoons lemon juice
3 egg yolks	2¼ cups olive oil

In a mortar, crush the garlic cloves with the salt to make a paste. Work in the egg yolks, pepper, and lemon juice. Proceed to drip in the olive oil, proceeding as in the instructions for Leslie's Mayonnaise (preceding). Serve with the Shellfish Platter or with chilled poached fish and/or an assortment of chilled fresh vegetables (raw and blanched).   *Makes 2½ to 3 cups.*

SPICY SQUASH SOUP

This is a lovely, lively soup made all the tastier with nutty croutons.

3 tablespoons butter	¼ teaspoon dry mustard
2 medium onions, chopped	2 tablespoons sesame seeds
1 bay leaf	4 cups peeled and finely chopped winter squash
1 whole clove garlic	
½ to 1 teaspoon ground pasilla pepper (or chili powder) to taste	1 cup orange juice
1 teaspoon turmeric	1 quart chicken broth (or other light stock)
1 teaspoon fenugreek leaves (not seeds)	2½ cups milk, more or less
½ teaspoon allspice	Cashew Croutons (recipe follows)
½ teaspoon ginger	

Melt butter in a large pot and sauté onions slowly over low heat. Add bay leaf, garlic, pepper (or chili powder), turmeric, fenugreek leaves, allspice, ginger, mustard, and sesame seeds. Cook over low heat, stirring, for 5 minutes. Add squash, orange juice, and broth. Cover and cook until squash is falling apart (about 1½ hours). Purée in a blender, strain, and return to pot. Stir in milk, using enough to reach the desired consistency. Garnish with Cashew Croutons. *Makes 8 to 10 servings.*

CASHEW CROUTONS

Do try these croutons. As someone said, they are "croutons worth fighting for."

3 tablespoons butter	Zest of 2 large limes,
1 cup coarsely chopped	shredded
raw cashews	2 cups firm whole
	wheat bread cubes

Melt butter and fry cashews until browned. Remove cashews with slotted spoon and combine in a bowl with the lime zest. Fry the bread cubes in the remaining butter until nicely toasted, and combine with the cashew-lime mixture. Sprinkle over bowls of hot soup just before serving. *Makes approximately 3 cups.*

GRILLED LEG OF LAMB THE VERY BEST WAY

This is indeed an excellent way to serve lamb. In addition, the different thicknesses mean that some of the meat will be rarer and some a little more done, allowing everyone's taste to be satisfied. You may use one of Leslie's marinades or another of your own choice — perhaps one of the others included in this collection.

1 whole leg of lamb (as close to tubular and as far from triangular as possible), boned to make a single flat piece	Choice of Yogurt-Orange or Mixed-Herb marinades (recipes below)

Place marinade of choice in a large baking dish, and marinate the boned lamb in the refrigerator for 12 to 24 hours. Let it come to room temperature, then take it out of the marinade and wipe it dry. (If the surface is damp, it won't sear properly.)

Prepare the grill. The coals should be red-hot with a coating of ash. Pare a piece of fat from the meat, impale it on a long fork, and rub it over the grill. Place the flattened lamb on the grill and sear it for 2 or 3 minutes on each side. Raise the grill 4 or 5 inches, using bricks if necessary to get the desired height. Continue to cook the meat for 5 to 8 minutes more on each side, basting with the marinade. Judge for doneness as for steak — the lamb should be nice and pink inside. This lamb can also be broiled; broil on a preheated pan 4 to 8 inches from heat — just as if using a grill. *Serves 2 to 3 per pound.*

YOGURT-ORANGE MARINADE

The orange marmalade and cumin give this marinade a distinctive flavor, similar to that of some Mexican cooking.

2 cups plain yogurt	1 tablespoon orange
1 onion, finely minced	marmalade
Juice of 1 orange	2 teaspoons ground
3 cloves garlic, crushed	cumin

Combine ingredients and use as marinade for lamb, chicken, or other meat. *Makes 2½ to 3 cups.*

MIXED-HERB MARINADE

This is the more classic butterflied lamb marinade.

½ cup olive oil	Strip of lemon peel (1
¼ cup red wine vinegar	by 2 inches)
2 cloves garlic, crushed	½ teaspoon each
1 carrot, chopped	peppercorns and
1 onion, chopped	sugar
1 tablespoon snipped	3 whole cloves
fresh marjoram or 1	2 bay leaves
teaspoon dried	

Combine ingredients and use as marinade for lamb, pork, chicken, or other meat. *Makes about 1½ cups.*

PORK SATÉ WITH PEANUT SAUCE

In Indonesian cooking, a saté *means grilled cured meat cooked on skewers.*

Lean cut of pork (loin, leg, or shoulder), allowing 8 to 12 ounces per person	Peanut Sauce/Marinade (recipe follows) Thin bamboo skewers

Cut the pork into 1½-inch cubes, allowing 8 to 10 cubes per person. Bring a large kettle of lightly salted water to a boil, add the pork cubes, and let them sit for 1 minute. Drain the meat and spread it out to cool lightly covered. Make Peanut Sauce/Marinade and mix with cooled pork cubes, making sure each piece is coated. Marinate in the refrigerator overnight, or up to 2 days.

When ready to serve, make a charcoal fire, one that will provide a good bed of coals. Soak the bamboo skewers in cold water for about an hour, then thread the pork cubes onto the skewers, about 4 cubes on each. Catch any sauce that drips off and combine it with any left in the bowl, adding enough water to make a sauce that you can spoon over the meat as it cooks (the sauce should have the consistency of thick applesauce). Put the grilling rack about 6 inches above the fire, let it get hot, then place the skewers on the rack. Cook for 5 minutes, then turn over. Cook another 10 minutes, until the underside is quite brown, then turn again and start basting with the sauce. Keep turning and basting for 10 to 15 minutes longer, until the juice from a cut piece flows clear and the sauce crust is firm.

Serve with roasted yams, skewered pineapple and peach pieces that can also be grilled, and a platter of raw vegetables to nibble on while the meat cooks.

PEANUT SAUCE/MARINADE

Be careful when adding the hot pepper to this sauce — not everyone can take the greater amount!

1 pound salted crunchy-style peanut butter (freshly ground, without extra oil)	3 or 4 large cloves garlic, crushed
½ cup dry sherry	Pinch of powdered ginger
⅓ cup tamari or other aged soy sauce	1 teaspoon to 2 tablespoons crushed red hot pepper to taste
¼ cup brown sugar	

To make the sauce/marinade, put peanut butter into a deep bowl. Work in the sherry (mixture will be stiff). Stir in the tamari. Add the brown sugar, crushed garlic, ginger, and hot pepper (2 tablespoons will make it extremely hot). Mix together well and use to coat saté. *Makes 2½ to 3 cups, enough for 4 to 6 servings.*

LIMPA MUFFINS

These uniquely flavored muffins are good two ways — hot fresh from the oven and leftover, toasted.

1 cup all-purpose flour	1 teaspoon caraway seeds
1 cup rye flour	1 egg, beaten
1 tablespoon baking powder	¼ cup molasses
½ teaspoon salt	1 cup minus 2 tablespoons milk
2 teaspoons grated orange zest	¼ cup butter, melted

Combine flours, baking powder, and salt; stir in orange zest and caraway seeds. In a separate bowl, combine egg, molasses, milk, and butter. Butter a dozen muffin cups and preheat oven to 375°F. Combine the liquid and dry ingredients with a few swift strokes — don't worry about a few lumps. Distribute the batter among the cups, smoothing out any floury lumps. Bake for 20 to 25 minutes or until well browned. Serve at once. Any leftovers can be split and toasted before serving. *Makes 12 medium-sized muffins.*

RICH EGG BREAD

This versatile dough is rich, satiny and handles beautifully. The baked products have a fine, light texture and an elegant flavor.

1½ tablespoons active dry yeast	1 tablespoon sugar
¼ cup warm water (105° to 115° F.)	9 cups bread flour (approximately), divided
2 cups light cream	¾ cup soft butter
5 large eggs	1 egg, beaten
2 teaspoons salt	2 tablespoons milk

In a bread bowl, dissolve yeast in the warm water. When the yeast foams, beat in the cream, eggs, salt, and sugar. Beat in 3 cups of flour, then the butter, then enough additional flour (about 6 more cups) to make a soft, slightly sticky dough. Knead thoroughly, cover, and let rise slowly in the refrigerator overnight or for about 15 hours. Punch down, knead briefly, shape, and let rise in a warm place until doubled. Beat the egg with the milk and brush mixture on the bread just before baking. Bake at 375°F. until golden brown. This amount of dough makes 3 standard-sized loaves of bread. Vary the shapes by making a braided wreath, rolls (either freehand or in muffin tins), or Babas (see recipe below). Times will vary. *Makes 3 large loaves or 1 large braided loaf, 8 rolls, 1 small loaf, and a dozen babas.*

BABAS

Measure 1½ cups of the raw Rich Egg Bread dough (above) after the first rising, when it is punched down. Knead in 1 tablespoon sugar, 1 teaspoon grated lemon zest, and ½ cup currants or chopped raisins. Half-fill well-buttered baba or other small molds, let rise until doubled, and bake at 400°F. until golden brown. Soak in syrup (recipe follows) for at least 4 hours, or up to a month, at which point they will be completely soggy but still delicious. Serve with vanilla ice cream. *Makes 12.*

SYRUP FOR BABAS: Combine 1½ cups sugar with ¾ cup water. Cook, stirring constantly, over low heat until sugar melts, then simmer for 5 minutes or until a medium syrup is formed. Let cool, then add ½ cup rum, brandy, or applejack. Syrup may also be flavored with vanilla or citrus zest.

PEARS IN WINE

A truly sumptuous dessert, guaranteed to transport even the most inexperienced cook to master chefdom — if only for a single night.

Use Seckels or underripe Boscs. Peel, leaving stems on, and store in acidulated water until ready to use, so that pears won't turn brown (to acidulate water, add the juice of 1 lemon for every half-gallon water). Mix a wine of your choice with equal quantities of fresh water to make enough liquid to cover the pears completely (2 quarts total liquid, including water, covers about 8 pears). Measure the liquid and add 3 tablespoons sugar for each cup. Season (see below for suggestions) and bring the liquid to a simmer. Cook uncovered for about 10 minutes, then add pears. Poach gently until the pears are tender (it will take 20 minutes to 2 hours, depending on the pears — test with a sharp knife point). Remove the pears and boil the liquid until it is reduced to a medium-weight syrup. Taste and add sugar if necessary. Pour the syrup over the pears and marinate for at least 2 hours, but not more than 4 or 5 days. (To get the red pears evenly and darkly red, keep turning them and marinate for several days.) To serve, cut a thin slice from the bottom of each pear so it will stand upright, and serve with crisp, not-too-sweet cookies.

Seasoning Suggestions: With white wine, use either a 3- or 4-inch strip of lemon zest and a ½-inch slice of fresh ginger, *or* half a vanilla bean. With red wine, use a 3- or 4-inch strip of orange peel and a 2-inch piece of stick cinnamon (remove the cinnamon after 1 day, or the flavor will be too strong).

Phyllis Siebert at the Blaine House sink.

Cooking at Blaine House

PHYLLIS SIEBERT
Augusta, Maine

Only a little north of Leslie Land on Route 95, Phyllis Siebert is also busily cooking "fancy foods" — fancy, plain, and everything in between . . . and at all times. Phyllis is the head cook at Blaine House, the official mansion of Maine's governor.

As this is written, Phyllis's present "easy to please" boss is Joseph E. Brennan. However, over the nearly 12 years that she has been at her job in Augusta, Phyllis has had to please several different bosses — each with different tastes and different schedules: no easy task. Not only does Phyllis have to adjust her cooking to meet the tastes of the varied administrations, she must also be prepared to please the palates of the mansion's many guests.

But despite the constraints of a budget determined by the state legislature, and the unsettled comings and goings (unexpected luncheon and supper guests are the norm, mealtimes are shuffled as frequently as cards, and less frequently, thank heavens, as many as 50 can arrive unexpectedly for tea), Phyllis loves her job. She especially likes the opportunity to improvise as the variety of occasions allows — and demands.

There are, of course, certain givens to Phyllis's job: there will always be a fair number of official receptions when "fancy food" is as expected as pine trees in the Pine Tree State (fortunately she has help from the seven-member staff who keep Blaine House running), and there will always be a lot of lobster served. (Visiting dignitaries expect lobster when in Maine, even though few know how to cope with the beast properly. Phyllis solves this by removing

199

the meat, cutting it into bite-sized pieces, tucking it back into the shell, and then reheating it briefly before serving.) There will also always be lots of Maine potatoes (the governor prefers his baked with butter). Then, too, there is always the annual Christmas Cookie Bake (you'll learn more about that in the recipe section). These "givens" Phyllis also enjoys.

However, Phyllis's cooking doesn't stop at the mansion's dining room door. In addition to looking after the culinary needs of the governor, his two teenage daughters, and the extended official family, she has two other "families" to tend to: there is the staff family, and, of course, her own personal family — her husband, Otto, and daughter, Kim.

But you needn't run for governor of Maine to enjoy one of the job's main perquisites — Phyllis's cooking. A sampling of the recipes loved by all three of Phyllis's families is here for you to try.

EXCELSIOR SOUP

This is a lovely, creamy soup — its warm coral color just right for a cold winter's day in Maine or elsewhere.

1 can (16 ounces) corn	Salt to taste
1 onion, sliced	Paprika to taste
½ cup chopped celery	¼ cup butter
3 pints chicken or veal stock	¼ cup flour
1 can (16 ounces) tomatoes	1 pint half-and-half

Combine corn, onion, celery, and stock in a soup kettle and simmer for 30 minutes. Add tomatoes and cook for 15 minutes longer. Press through a food mill or sieve, then return mixture to soup kettle. Add salt and paprika. In a small saucepan, melt butter, whisk in flour, and add half-and-half. Add to the puréed vegetable mixture. Heat to boiling and serve at once. *Makes 6 to 7 cups.*

DILLED POTATO AND CUCUMBER SOUP

It's good to know that this favorite of so many households is also a favored dish at Maine's Blaine House. Pickle lovers may disagree, but can there be a better way to honor each summer's cucumber crop?

1 cup chopped onion	2 to 3 tablespoons fresh
4 cups sliced raw	dill, chopped, or 1½
potatoes	to 2 teaspoons dried
3 cups water	Salt and freshly ground
1 medium cucumber,	black pepper to taste
peeled and chopped	Freshly chopped chives
2 cups milk	or scallions, for
1 cup sour cream	garnish

Place onion, potatoes, and water in a soup kettle or large saucepan and simmer until potatoes are soft. Cool to room temperature. Purée in a blender, gradually adding pieces of cucumber. Blend until very smooth. Return to kettle and whisk in milk, then whisk in sour cream until uniformly blended. Add dill. Chill well. Taste and season with salt and pepper. Serve garnished with chives or scallions. *Makes 6 to 7 generous servings.*

FRUIT SOUP

A wonderfully versatile soup. Served as described here, it makes a refreshing appetizer or hot-weather cooler; sweetened a bit more and topped with a bit of whipped cream, it makes a delicious light dessert.

3 cups unsweetened
   orange, apple, or
   pineapple juice
1 banana
1 apple, peeled and
   chopped
1 peach, peeled and
   chopped
Pieces of fresh
   cantaloupe
½ teaspoon dried mint

Juice of 1 lemon
2 tablespoons honey,
   more or less to taste
1 cup yogurt, sour
   cream, or buttermilk
Dash of cinnamon,
   nutmeg, or allspice
Fresh mint leaf, violet,
   or rose petal, for
   garnish

Combine all ingredients except for garnish in a blender and purée until smooth. Thicken with additional banana or yogurt; thin, if desired, with more fruit juice. Chill thoroughly. Garnish each serving with a dollop of yogurt or sour cream and a fresh mint leaf, violet, or rose petal.   *Makes 6 cups.*

BLUEFISH WITH PORTUGAISE SAUCE

Maine's governor, like most of us, is concerned about cholesterol, so Phyllis serves a good bit of fish. She fashions her recipe for this bluefish dish after one Marion Morash suggests for swordfish in her Victory Garden Cookbook.

4 to 5 pounds bluefish
3 tablespoons olive oil
1 cup sliced scallions or milk onions
Dash of Tabasco sauce
2 teaspoons minced garlic
3 cups chopped tomato pulp
3 tablespoons capers
1 tablespoon red wine vinegar
1 bay leaf
2 whole cloves
½ teaspoon Worcestershire sauce
Salt and pepper to taste
Flour for dredging fish
4 tablespoons butter
Lemon wedges, for garnish

Fillet bluefish and remove skin. Set aside. Heat olive oil in a large skillet and sauté scallions or onions until translucent. Add Tabasco and garlic. Add tomato pulp, capers, vinegar, bay leaf, cloves, Worcestershire sauce, salt, and pepper, and simmer 20 to 30 minutes. Dredge bluefish in flour. Heat butter in skillet and brown fish, cooking gently until nearly done. Place fillets in a large baking dish, top each piece with some of the sauce, and cover with foil. Bake about 20 minutes at 350°F. Garnish with lemon wedges and serve. The fish can be held in warm oven if meal is delayed.

Serves 8 for dinner, more for lunch.

PHYLLIS'S SOUR CREAM COFFEE CAKE

Since the morning coffee hour is a popular time for informal meetings — and even tours (with refreshments) — at Blaine House, there is usually a coffee cake baking in Phyllis's oven first thing each day. This sour cream cake is one of her favorites. It's a moist, finely textured cake with a rich, buttery taste.

1 cup butter	1 teaspoon baking
2 cups plus 4 teaspoons	powder
sugar	¼ teaspoon salt
2 eggs	1 cup coarsely chopped
1 cup sour cream	pecans
½ teaspoon vanilla	1 teaspoon cinnamon
2 cups flour	

Cream butter with 2 cups of the sugar. One at a time, beat in the eggs. Fold in the sour cream and vanilla. Sift together the flour, baking powder, and salt, and mix in. Place batter in a greased 9- by 13-inch cake pan. Combine pecans, cinnamon, and the remaining 4 teaspoons sugar and sprinkle on top of batter. Bake at 350°F. for about 40 to 45 minutes or until cake tests done.

Makes 10 to 12 pieces.

ALMOND ROLL

The almonds add a welcome fresh flavor to this roll, and the airy berry filling gives the whole a fluffy lightness not found in the more usual jelly roll. However, the dessert does slither a bit when served; be sure to have a sharp-edged, broad-based cake knife handy.

7 eggs	½ cup fresh or frozen
¾ cup sugar	strawberrries, mashed
1½ cups ground	Confectioners' sugar, for
almonds	dusting
1 teaspoon baking	Fresh strawberries, for
powder	garnish (optional)
1 cup heavy cream	

Line a jelly-roll pan with waxed paper; oil the paper. Separate the eggs. With a heavy whisk, beat the yolks with the sugar until the mixture ribbons. Beat in the ground almonds and the baking powder. Beat the egg whites until stiff and gently fold into the almond mixture. Spread the batter out on the oiled paper. Bake at 350°F. for 15 to 20 minutes. Cool in pan, then cover (the cake still in the pan) with a damp cloth and chill. Just before serving, whip the cream and fold in the mashed berries. Dust the top of the cake with confectioners' sugar and turn it out onto a towel. Remove the waxed paper. Spread the surface of the cake with the strawberry whipped cream. Roll the cake and place on a platter. Dust with confectioners' sugar and garnish with fresh berries, if available.

Serves 10.

COLD CHOCOLATE SOUFFLÉ
WITH RASPBERRY SAUCE

Is there anyone "with soul so dead" who doesn't love the mixture of chocolate and raspberry? This soufflé is no exception: the rich chocolate and slightly tart raspberry flavors are meant for each other.

4 whole eggs plus 3 egg
    yolks
½ cup sugar
1½ tablespoons
    unflavored gelatin
¼ cup water
2 teaspoons orange juice
5 ounces dark sweet
    chocolate

½ ounce unsweetened
    chocolate
3 tablespoons strong
    coffee
2 tablespoons brandy
½ cup heavy cream
Raspberry Sauce (recipe
    follows)

Combine whole eggs, egg yolks, and sugar in a 2-quart bowl, and beat for 15 minutes with an electric mixer. Soften the gelatin in a mixture of the water and orange juice; dissolve over hot water and let cool. Melt the chocolate in a heavy pan with the coffee and brandy. Add the cooled gelatin and melted chocolate mixture to the beaten eggs and mix well. Whip the cream to soft peaks and fold in. Oil a 6-inch band of waxed paper and tie it around the rim of a 1-quart soufflé dish to form a collar. Fill the dish with the soufflé mixture to about 3 inches above the rim and chill until set. Remove the paper. If desired, press shredded sweet chocolate around the exposed sides of the soufflé. Serve with Raspberry Sauce. *Makes 10 to 12 servings.*

RASPBERRY SAUCE

This raspberry sauce would no doubt make an excellent topping for many other of the puddings and mousses in this collection (especially the lemon). It's certainly perfection here.

1 cup raspberry juice (from fresh or frozen berries)	1 cup water 4 tablespoons sugar 2 teaspoons cornstarch

Bring juice, water, and sugar to a boil. Add cornstarch dissolved in enough water to make a thick paste. Cook until slightly thickened. Cool before serving. *Makes about 2 cups.*

ETHEL'S SUGAR COOKIES

This is the recipe — originally borrowed from the Betty Crocker Cookie Book *— Phyllis uses to make the Christmas cookies that Blaine House sends to the 1,000 Augusta-area Head Start children each year. She multiplies the recipe as needed in several big batches; then, as time permits, bakes up what she can. Another staff member decorates the cookies, after which they are hidden so that the staff — and who knows, maybe even the governor — can't find them before Christmas.*

¾ cup shortening (part butter) 1 cup sugar 2 eggs ½ teaspoon lemon flavoring or 1 teaspoon vanilla	2½ cups flour 1 teaspoon baking powder 1 teaspoon salt

Cream shortening and sugar; beat in eggs and flavoring. Combine flour, baking powder, and salt, and blend into egg mixture. Chill dough for at least 1 hour. Roll out dough to ⅛-inch thickness on a floured board. Cut into desired shapes and place on an ungreased cookie sheet. Bake for 6 to 8 minutes at 400°F., until cookies are a delicate golden color. *Makes about 4 dozen.*

Marian Gauthier in her 1730 farmhouse kitchen.

Beside the Beehive Oven

MARIAN GAUTHIER
Franklin, Connecticut

Anyone looking for even more elegant New England cookery need only go as far as Franklin, Connecticut, where it takes place nearly every day around the massive stone fireplace that is the heart of Marian and Charles Gauthier's 1730 farmhouse kitchen. At first glance, one might be fooled: the lovely colonial room — complete with beehive oven — is chock-a-block with Marian's extensive collection of antique churns, baskets, and other well-worn Americana — so much so that one might wonder where any cooking could be done.

It is in the adjoining pantry that Marian keeps the modern implements of her culinary trade — her mixer, dough table, and soup pots. And it's obvious, when tasting her fine food, that this room must see a lot of her time. It's in the pantry, too, that she stockpiles her ingredients, buying them in quantity on sale. (To give you just an inkling: Marian bought 16 five-pound bags of flour — Gold Medal was her choice — in just one fall.)

Baking is perhaps Marian's main culinary passion. It must be, for she and her daughters make 80 (count them — 80) different kinds of cookies each holiday season. She likes to bake things in at least double quantity so that she has something to freeze as well as to serve. ("Fillings freeze well," she tells us. However, "glazes should be added just before serving time.")

But Marian is also a champion soup and spaghetti maker. For the soup that is regular fare on the Gauthier wintertime supper table, Marian uses only ingredients that she herself has grown —

except for the sweet corn ("easily available at local farm stands") and the zucchini, which Marian has had "just too much of." For the spaghetti, she fries the meatballs in olive oil, then browns the tomato sauce and garlic in the same oil before adding them to the sauce, and of course, Marian uses only fresh herbs.

Almost as much as Marian loves baking and cooking, she loves reading about them. Her collection of old and new recipe books totals more than 300. ("I read cookbooks like novels — cover to cover.") Visiting with Marian in her beautiful colonial kitchen, one gets the feeling that she may well cook up almost every recipe before she's through. A few of her favorites follow here for you to try.

BEAN AND VEGETABLE SOUP

This soup takes a little more time to prepare, but it's well worth the effort: the vegetables are not overcooked. Serve immediately while the peas are still a bright green. With a salad and some bread, this substantial soup is ample for a light winter supper. Also, without the beef granules, it would make a fine vegetarian dish.

8 cups cold water	1 can (28 ounces)
1¼ cups dried navy	tomatoes, cut up
beans	1 cup chopped onion
2 tablespoons instant	½ cup sliced carrots
beef bouillon	½ cup chopped celery
granules	1 cup tiny shell
1 teaspoon sugar	macaroni
1 teaspoon dried thyme	1 package (10 ounces)
1 large bay leaf	frozen peas
½ teaspoon salt, or	1 can (8 ounces) whole
more to taste	kernel corn
⅛ teaspoon pepper	

Place water and navy beans in a 4-quart Dutch oven. Bring to a boil and simmer for 2 minutes. Remove from heat. Cover and let stand for 1 hour. Add bouillon, sugar, thyme, bay leaf, salt, and pepper. Bring to a boil; reduce heat and simmer, covered, for 1 hour. Add tomatoes, onions, carrots, and celery, and simmer for an additional 20 minutes, covered. Add macaroni and cook for 10 minutes more. Remove bay leaf. Stir in peas and undrained corn. Heat to boiling, just long enough to cook peas.

Makes 8 to 10 substantial servings.

CHINESE CHICKEN WINGS

These sweet-and-sour chicken wings make a nice main dish served with rice and the trimmings. Dried out a bit, they would also make a tempting hors d'oeuvre.

5 pounds chicken wings	3 tablespoons vinegar
1 stick (½ cup) butter or margarine	5 tablespoons brown sugar
4 cloves garlic, crushed	⅓ cup water
3 tablespoons ketchup	

In a large skillet, brown wings in butter and garlic. When wings are almost brown, remove garlic and fry wings until they are completely browned on all sides. (Depending on size of your skillet, you may need to do this in batches.) Set aside. In a small saucepan, combine ketchup, vinegar, brown sugar, and water. Bring to a boil. Pour over wings and simmer for 10 minutes over low heat.

Serves 6 to 8.

CHEESE-FILLED CHICKEN CUTLETS

The chicken in these cutlets is tender and moist, and its gentle flavor is not challenged by the mild cheese. The mushroom white sauce is just right. Skewering the cutlets together is tricky; it may take a little practice.

3 whole chicken breasts	½ pound mushrooms,
¼ teaspoon salt	thinly sliced
4 tablespoons flour,	⅛ teaspoon pepper
divided	½ cup water
5 tablespoons butter,	½ cup milk
divided	¼ cup white wine
1 package (8 ounces)	1 chicken bouillon cube
mozzarella cheese,	Parsley sprigs, for
thinly sliced	garnish

Bone and skin the chicken breasts. Cut each whole breast in half and cut each half into 2 cutlets. Pound each cutlet to about ⅛-inch thick. Mix salt with 3 tablespoons flour and coat chicken with this mixture. In a skillet, melt 3 tablespoons butter, add cutlets a few at a time, and sauté until lightly browned on both sides, adding more butter if necessary. Remove cutlets from the skillet. Arrange cheese slices on 6 cutlets; top with remaining cutlets and skewer layers together with toothpicks. Set aside. In the drippings, melt the remaining 2 tablespoons butter. Add mushrooms and cook until tender, stirring occasionally. Stir in pepper and the remaining 1 tablespoon flour; blend well. Gradually stir in water, milk, wine, and bouillon. Heat to boiling, stirring to loosen brown bits from the bottom of the skillet. Return cutlets to skillet; heat to boiling. Reduce heat to low; cover and simmer for 5 minutes or until cheese is melted. Carefully remove toothpicks. Spoon cutlets and sauce onto a large platter; garnish with parsley sprigs. *Makes 6 servings.*

BUTTERCRUST FLAKE-APARTS
Fan Tans

When done, these slightly sweet rolls are the match of any bakery fan-tan dinner roll. The shaping is easy but looks fancy, and the texture is moist and firm.

4¼ to 5 cups all-purpose flour
⅓ cup sugar
2 teaspoons salt
½ teaspoon baking soda
2 packages (scant tablespoon each) active dry yeast

1½ cups buttermilk or sour milk
½ cup butter plus 2 tablespoons melted butter

In a large mixer bowl, combine 2 cups flour, sugar, salt, soda, and yeast. In a saucepan, heat buttermilk and ½ cup butter until buttermilk is warm (butter does not need to melt). Add to flour mixture. Blend with mixer at lowest speed until moistened, then beat for 2 minutes at medium speed. By hand, stir in the remaining flour to make a stiff dough. Cover and let rise in a warm place until light and doubled in size (about 1 hour). Punch down dough. On a floured board, roll out dough to a 15-inch square. Brush with 2 tablespoons melted butter, and cut dough into 1½-inch-wide strips. Stack 5 strips together and cut into stacks 1½ inches long. Place cut-side down in greased muffin cups. Cover and let rise until doubled (about 30 minutes). Bake at 400°F. for 15 to 20 minutes, until golden brown. Serve warm.   *Makes about 20 rolls.*

PECAN STREUSEL COFFEE CAKE

This superior cinnamon-flavored not-too-sweet coffee cake receives a 10-plus rating everywhere it goes. The bread-crumb streusel is tastier, adheres better, and is much more reminiscent of the original European streusels than those we usually meet. Don't worry if the dough coils seem skimpy in the pans: they will expand to fill.

1 recipe Basic Sweet Dough (see recipe following)

FILLING:

1 cup brown sugar	Dash of salt
½ cup butter, softened	½ cup chopped pecans
1 tablespoon cinnamon	

TOPPING:

½ cup fine dry bread crumbs	½ teaspoon vanilla
½ cup granulated sugar	½ cup pecan halves, more or less, for
¼ cup butter, softened	garnish

CONFECTIONERS' SUGAR ICING:

1 cup confectioners' sugar	1 to 2 tablespoons milk
	½ teaspoon vanilla

Let Sweet Dough rise in a warm place until doubled, about 1½ hours. Meanwhile, mix all filling ingredients together, blend well, and set aside. Punch down dough; divide into thirds. On a lightly floured board, roll each third into a 6- by 18-inch rectangle. Spread each rectangle with one-third of the filling. Starting at the long side, roll up as for a jelly roll; seal edges. Work each roll with your hands to about a 24-inch length. Grease 3 round 9-inch cake pans and coil 1 roll loosely in each pan, pinching the ends of the roll together. Cover pans and let dough rise until double, 45 to 60 minutes. Mix together all topping ingredients, except pecan halves. Sprinkle one-third of the topping over each coil. Bake at 375°F. for 20 to 25 minutes. Just before serving, mix Confectioners' Sugar Icing, drizzle it over the cakes, and top with reserved pecan halves.

Makes three 9-inch coffee cakes, each serving 8 to 10.

BASIC SWEET DOUGH

This is a wonderfully moist basic yeast dough with great flavor and texture. It is, however, a very soft dough and sometimes requires a little chilling before handling.

2 packages (scant tablespoon each) active dry yeast	½ cup shortening
	½ cup sugar
	1½ teaspoons salt
½ cup warm water (105° to 115°F.)	5 to 5½ cups flour
	3 eggs
¾ cup milk	

Sprinkle yeast over water; set aside to proof. In a small saucepan, heat milk, shortening, sugar, and salt until warm (shortening does not need to melt). Pour into a large mixer bowl; beat in 2 cups flour until well mixed. Add yeast mixture and eggs. Beat, scraping bowl occasionally. Add ½ cup additional flour and beat well; then add enough of the remaining flour (you will likely need it all) to make a soft dough. Turn out onto a lightly floured surface. Knead for 8 to 10 minutes, until dough is smooth and satiny. Place in a greased bowl; turn to grease top. Cover dough and proceed with Pecan Streusel Coffee Cake or a variation of your own choice.

Makes ample dough for three 9-inch coffee cakes.

NEW ENGLAND RAISIN BREAD

This hearty raisin bread is especially good toasted — a real man pleaser. The loaves are very large; depending on your needs, you might prefer to make three smaller loaves, adjusting the temperature and timing as needed.

2 packages (scant tablespoon each) active dry yeast	¼ cup sugar
	1 tablespoon salt
½ cup warm water	3 eggs
1½ cups lukewarm milk (scalded, then cooled)	¼ cup butter, softened
	7 to 7½ cups flour
	2 cups raisins

Dissolve yeast in warm water. Stir in milk, sugar, salt, eggs, butter, and about 3½ cups of the flour; beat until smooth. Mix in raisins and enough of the remaining flour to make the dough easy to handle. Knead the dough on a floured board until smooth and elastic (about 10 minutes). Place in a greased bowl and turn to grease the top. Cover and let rise until doubled, about 1½ hours. Punch down and divide the dough in half. Roll each half into a rectangle and then roll up to form a loaf. Seal the seam and fold the ends under. Place loaves seam-side down in large greased bread pans and let rise until double. Heat oven to 400°F. Bake breads on the middle rack for 25 to 30 minutes, until golden brown. If breads appear to brown too quickly, cover tops of loaves with foil for the final 15 minutes or so of the baking time. (Loaves should sound hollow when tapped.) Remove from pans and cool on wire racks. Brush with butter if desired or frost with Confectioners' Sugar Icing (just preceding). *Makes 2 loaves.*

ENGLISH MUFFIN BREAD

This coarse-textured bread is reminiscent of English muffins. Knead it as little as possible, since kneading develops a finer texture.

1 cup milk	1 package (scant
2 tablespoons sugar	tablespoon) active dry
1 teaspoon salt	yeast
3 tablespoons butter or	5½ cups flour
margarine	(approximately)
1 cup warm water	Cornmeal

Scald milk; stir in sugar, salt, and butter. Cool to lukewarm. Pour the warm water into a large warmed bowl and sprinkle in yeast. Stir until dissolved. Stir in lukewarm milk mixture. Add 3 cups flour; beat until smooth. Add enough additional flour to make a soft dough. Turn out onto a floured board; knead for 2 minutes or less, just until dough can be formed into a ball. (Dough may be slightly sticky.) Place in a greased bowl; turn to grease top. Cover and let rise until doubled, about 1 hour. Punch down dough; divide in half. Shape into 2 loaves. Roll each loaf in cornmeal. Place in greased 4- by 8-inch loaf pans. Cover and let rise until doubled, up to 1 hour. Bake at 400°F. for 20 minutes or so until done. Remove from baking pans; cool on wire racks. Slice and toast like English muffins. *Makes 2 loaves.*

MOST DIVINE TRIPLE-CHOCOLATE PIE

This luscious chocolate — mocha, really — pie is indeed divine. The bittersweet filling is a perfect complement to the rich shell and bland cream topping.

CHOCOLATE SHELL:

⅓ cup shortening
1 cup flour
¼ teaspoon salt

½ square (½ ounce)
  semisweet chocolate,
  grated
2 tablespoons water

Cut shortening into flour and salt. Stir in grated chocolate. Sprinkle water over mixture and blend lightly until dough holds together. Roll out dough and line a 9-inch pie plate; flute edge. Weight shell (pie beans are good for this) and bake at 400°F. for about 12 minutes or until firm.

CHOCOLATE FILLING:

1 envelope (1
  tablespoon)
  unflavored gelatin
¼ cup sugar, plus ¼ cup
  for meringue
¼ teaspoon salt
1 teaspoon instant
  coffee powder
1 cup milk
3 eggs, separated

3 squares (1 ounce each)
  unsweetened
  chocolate
½ teaspoon vanilla
¼ teaspoon cream of
  tartar
2 cups whipping cream
½ (½ ounce) square
  semisweet chocolate,
  grated

Mix gelatin, ¼ cup sugar, salt, and instant coffee powder in a large heavy saucepan. Blend in milk and beaten egg yolks, then add unsweetened chocolate. Heat slowly, stirring constantly, until chocolate is melted and the mixture starts to thicken (don't let it boil). Pour into a large bowl; add vanilla and stir until smooth and blended. Cool until mixture "mounds" (holds its shape). Beat egg whites with cream of tartar until foamy; then beat in the remaining

¼ cup sugar, a tablespoon at a time, until meringue stands in stiff peaks. In a second bowl, using the same beaters, beat 1 cup cream until stiff. Beat the cooled chocolate mixture until smooth; fold in meringue, then fold in whipped cream. Pour into the baked chocolate shell. Chill until firm. Beat remaining 1 cup whipping cream until stiff. Mound onto pie. Sprinkle grated semisweet chocolate over the cream.   *Makes 8 to 10 servings.*

SEMISWEET CRESCENTS

Another addictive cookie that few of us need but all of us love. This dough handles beautifully and could be rolled into smaller crescents, if you prefer.

½ cup semisweet
   chocolate pieces
1 tablespoon milk
2 cups flour
½ teaspoon salt
¾ cup butter, at room
   temperature

½ cup granulated sugar
2 teaspoons vanilla
½ cup chopped
   blanched almonds

In a small saucepan over hot (not boiling) water, melt chocolate pieces with milk; cool slightly. Sift flour with salt. Start heating the oven to 350°F. In a mixer bowl, beat butter at medium speed until creamy, then beat in sugar and vanilla until light and fluffy. Add melted chocolate. Beat in flour mixture gradually until thoroughly blended. Stir in almonds. Shape pieces of dough the size of a rounded teaspoon into crescents (the dough will roll into cylinders about 3 inches long) and place on ungreased cookie sheets. Bake for 12 to 15 minutes, keeping a careful watch. Let crescents set on pan a minute or two; then cool on wire racks and store in a tightly covered container.   *Makes 3 dozen.*

219

Minnie Biggs in front of her copper pot collection.

Enthusiasm: The Essential Ingredient

MINNIE BIGGS
Rockport, Maine

Emerson wrote: "Nothing great was ever achieved without enthusiasm," and enthusiasm is certainly high on the basic ingredient list of the Great New England Cooks you're meeting as you travel the pages of this book. Minnie Biggs is no exception; in fact, her enthusiasm cupboard is overflowing. Whether it be making picture-perfect French bread, freezing soul-satisfying ice cream, concocting dishes for her beloved coriander and hot peppers, gardening in her raised vegetable beds, or working for the Bay Chamber Concert series she helped found, Minnie greets it with enthusiasm — and it pays. Her French bread is locally renowned, her raised-bed garden made it to the semifinals of the annual WGBH (Boston public television) Victory Garden Contest in 1980, and the winter concert series continues to thrive.

Minnie came lately to cooking, but a job in Italy changed that. There, in large measure aided by an Italian beau, she learned to appreciate good food and to put it together properly. Back in the United States, and again aided by appreciative males — a "dear Greek bachelor friend" and, of course, her husband, Stephen (no mean cook himself) — Minnie's interest in good cooking flourished. Recently, her more traditional French/Continental cooking style has been veering Easterly, trailing wafts of garlic ("I do love it"). But whether it's a haute cuisine dinner, a nouveau-Chinese menu, or an after-concert party, if it's Minnie Biggs's, it's done with enthusiasm.

221

EGYPTIAN PIZZA

What Minnie Biggs says about this spinach comestible is that it "looks like green rubber-soled shoes and tastes like heaven on earth." We leave the shoe allusion to you but certainly agree that the end result is mighty tasty and, cut up small, makes a lovely hors d'oeuvre.

2 packages chopped frozen spinach, thawed (fresh chopped spinach or beet greens may be substituted)
1 cup onion, finely chopped
1 cup celery, finely chopped
¼ cup chopped fresh parsley
2 tablespoons celery seed
2 tablespoons dried basil
1 tablespoon oregano
1 tablespoon dried marjoram
2 tablespoons dried coriander
1 teaspoon ground ginger
⅓ cup chopped garlic
Salt and pepper to taste
4 to 6 eggs
1 cup grated stale blue or cheddar cheese
Sesame seeds or poppy seeds or fine bread crumbs (about ½ cup)

Mix spinach and chopped vegetables together with the assorted herbs and spices. Add eggs and cheese and mix well. Spread in a 9-by 13½-inch pan. Top with sesame seeds, poppy seeds, or bread crumbs. Bake in slow oven (225° to 250°F.) for 4 to 5 hours. The spinach mixture will dry out and become like crackers or biscuits. Cut the pizza into squares when cool, and freeze if desired.

Makes 16 to 20 servings.

MILLIONAIRES' CHICKEN

The combined sauces give this chicken a unique character. A delightful, light entrée.

1 frying chicken (2½ or 3 pounds), or the equivalent in parts

1 head iceberg or other crisp-head lettuce

SAUCE 1:

4 tablespoons soy sauce
2 tablespoons honey
1 clove garlic, put through a press

¼ teaspoon M.S.G. (Ac'cent), if desired

SAUCE 2:

4 tablespoons peanut oil
2 scallions, chopped or sliced thin
4 slices fresh ginger, peeled and minced (about a heaping tablespoon)

1 teaspoon Szechwan pepper
½ teaspoon dried, crushed hot red pepper
1 bunch fresh coriander (optional)

Simmer the chicken in a small amount of water until it is very tender. Drain off the liquid and save for stock. When the chicken is cool enough to handle, remove all skin and bones and either shred or chop the meat. Set aside, covered and chilled.

Near serving time, shred the lettuce into very fine ribbons. Combine ingredients for Sauce 1 and let stand 10 minutes or so. Put ingredients for Sauce 2 in a small saucepan and simmer over medium heat for about 3 minutes. Then combine the sauces.

To serve, make a bed of the shredded lettuce, mixing in some coriander, if available. Arrange the shredded chicken on the greens, pour the sauce over everything, and garnish with more coriander. (For very large parties, this can be made with turkey breast; multiply the sauces by about 6.)   *Serves 6.*

223

MANGO CHUTNEY

A delicious chutney — and cheaper than store-bought! Minnie makes quantities of this when mangoes are in season, earmarking at least some of the jars for gift giving.

2 very fat or 3 smaller semiripe mangoes	¼ cup finely chopped garlic
2 to 2½ cups sugar ("some brown and some white")	1 teaspoon ground cloves
1 cup cider vinegar	2 small fresh hot peppers, seeded and
½ cup raisins	thinly sliced, or 2
¼ cup peeled, finely chopped fresh ginger	tablespoons dried, crumbled

Peel, pit, and chop the mangoes, combine them with the sugar, and let stand, covered, at room temperature overnight. Drain the liquid into a saucepan, holding back the mangoes. Add everything else to the juice and simmer for 30 minutes. Add mangoes, simmer 30 minutes more, stirring frequently as the mixture thickens, then pour into sterilized jars and process for 15 minutes in a boiling-water bath. *Yield: 2 or 3 small jars.*

FRENCH BREAD

Minnie Biggs's French Bread is one she has adapted from a recipe for Poilane Peasant bread in Bernard Clayton's Breads of France. *Though it takes three days to complete, each step is simple to accomplish — and well worth it!*

7 cups all-purpose unbleached flour	1 tablespoon nonfat dry milk
1 tablespoon active dry yeast, dissolved in 1 cup warm (105° to 115°F.) water	2 cups warm water
	1 teaspoon salt
	Cornmeal, for dusting

Day 1. Starter: Beat together 1 cup flour and the dissolved yeast, mixed with the nonfat dry milk, and let stand, covered, at room temperature for 12 to 24 hours.

Day 2. Sponge: Add 2 cups warm water and 3 cups unbleached flour to the starter and mix well. Again cover and let stand 12 to 24 hours.

Day 3. Rising and Baking: Add salt, then 3 more cups of flour, or up to 1 more cup until kneading texture is elastic and easy. Knead *well.* Let rise, covered, in a very large bowl until the dough is completely doubled (about 3 hours). Then form into 3 fat or 4 thinner long loaves freehand. Let the formed bread rise until fully doubled — 2 hours at least. Bake the loaves on cornmeal-sprinkled baking sheets.

Preheat oven to 425°F. Have handy a mist-sprayer filled with cool fresh water. Slash the tops of the risen loaves and spray them gently. Open the oven, spray inside, and insert the bread. Spray the oven again 2 minutes later, 2 minutes after that, and 2 minutes after *that,* for a total of 4 sprayings in the first 6 minutes (that's what gives the bread such a nice crust). Bake for a total of 37 minutes or until done by your favorite bread test. Cool on racks and enjoy promptly or freeze.   *Makes 3 or 4 loaves.*

FRUIT ICE CREAM OR SHERBET

Minnie Biggs makes her ice cream and sherbet in a Salton ice cream maker. Since the company no longer makes their small inexpensive ice cream maker, she wondered if it was fair to include the recipes here. The end results got such raves from our Yankee testers we decided to give you the recipes anyway and let you do the freezing your own way. One Yankee tester froze hers in ice cube trays until mushy, then whipped it with the wire whip of her mixer before returning to freeze until proper consistency. (Of course, you can also use a hand-cranked or electric ice cream freezer.)

> 2 cups puréed fresh strawberries, raspberries, or
>   blueberries (about 1 quart)
> ½ cup superfine sugar

FOR SHERBET:
> 2 egg whites

FOR ICE CREAM:
> 1 envelope (1 tablespoon) unflavored gelatin
> ¼ cup cold water
> 2 cups heavy cream
> Dash of fruit *eau-de-vie* (the clear distillate of fruit,
>   not "fruit-flavored brandy"); use Cointreau for
>   strawberries, Framboise with raspberries, Poir
>   Wilhelm for blueberries, Southern Comfort for
>   peaches and apricots

Pureé the fruit through a food mill to remove seeds, mix with sugar, and set the mixture aside, covered, for about 20 minutes. Then stir again.

For Sherbet: Whip the egg whites into stiff but still shiny peaks. Carefully but thoroughly mix them with the sweetened fruit and freeze according to your favorite directions for freezing sherbet.

For Ice Cream: Sprinkle the gelatin over the cold water to soften. Combine it with ½ cup of the cream and heat, stirring, until the gelatin is dissolved and completely mixed in. Then remove from the heat and combine with the rest of the cream. Chill, covered, until the mixture is cold, then combine it with the sweetened fruit and fruit distillate and freeze according to the directions you use for ice cream.

When sherbet or ice cream is frozen to your liking, let it mellow in the freezer at least an hour before serving, but don't expect either dessert to keep for a long time. Both are best if served within a day or two. *Makes 1 quart.*

OLIVE'S SHORTBREAD

This sinfully rich and buttery shortbread from an Irish cook of Minnie's early days is rather thicker than some but still beautifully baked through. If you should have trouble finding the rice flour, try a Chinese grocery or specialty shop — it is labeled "glutinous rice powder" and is called "sweet." Many shortbreads are made with sweet butter but this one is not.

| 1 cup salted butter | 2 cups unbleached flour |
| Scant ½ cup sugar | ½ cup fine rice flour |

Beat butter and sugar until very light and creamy. Add sifted flours and mix gently but thoroughly by hand. Pack into an ungreased 8- or 9-inch square tin. When the dough is smoothly packed, go around the sides with a thin-bladed spatula, running it between the dough and the walls of the pan. Cut dough all the way through into small rectangles, then prick each rectangle with the tines of a fork. Bake in a 325°F. oven for 50 or 55 minutes, until the shortbread is golden. Cut through again at the original markings while the cookies are still hot, but don't try to remove them from the pan until they cool.

Makes approximately thirty-two 1- by 2-inch rectangles.

Elaine Noyes . . . and pies.

A Profusion of Pies

ELAINE NOYES
Cornish, Maine

One year, Elaine Noyes thought she'd try to keep track of the pies she bakes for The Enterprise, the family restaurant in Cornish she and her former husband bought some 15 or so years ago. She gave up at 3,500. Today, Elaine's sisters and her daughter cook most of The Enterprise's menu, but in large measure it is the "Best Pies in All Maine" that draw people to the restaurant's door.

Genuinely puzzled by people who ask for her pie-baking secrets, Elaine claims to have only one — her mother. "I can't remember," she explains, "when there wasn't a pie baking in the oven." (Elaine obviously learned well.) Nonetheless, she was happy to share what she could of her steps to a tender pie shell.

As to ingredients, she much prefers Robin Hood flour and refuses any shortening other than Crisco. Beyond that, she uses a pastry blender to cut the shortening into the flour, stopping as soon as the mixture forms pea-sized, but still crumbly, lumps ("Never work the dough longer than you need to"). To add the *iced* water ("The colder the water, the crispier the crust"), she spoons out a hole in the center of the flour mixture and folds in the water from there with the spoon. "The water," Elaine explains, "keeps the fat from melting, but you don't want too much — just so you can mix it, that's all. If you don't have enough, it won't hold together to roll out; too much will make the crust too soft. When you can squeeze the dough," she continues, "and it just holds together, that's good pie crust."

When it comes to rolling out the dough, Elaine advises

flouring the board and pin very lightly. "You already have the right texture; the more flour you work into the dough, the tougher it will be." Elaine handles dough as little as possible ("You don't want hands in there melting the fat"), patting out what she needs into a rounded cake. She then rolls the crust out from the center as thin as possible — no thicker than ⅛ inch ("Any thicker and you might as well be making cookies . . . and never roll back and forth"). She spreads the crust loosely over the bottom of the pie plate (Elaine prefers Pyrex plates — "Shiny tin bottoms can burn crust"), trimming off any excess dough with a knife. She rolls out the top crust with equal care, spreads it lightly with additional Crisco and milk, sprinkles a bit of flour over all ("to brown it and make it flaky"), and vents it with small slits. The crust is then put in place and the pie tucked into the oven — started at a higher temperature for a short while ("The hot oven browns up the crust") and then cooked at reduced heat until done. The times and temperatures vary. (Elaine's basic two-crust pie pastry recipe immediately follows her Apple Pie.)

How better to wind down this collection of great New England recipes than with this splendid array of delicious pies — just as so many great New England meals also wind down.

APPLE PIE

Elaine never uses McIntosh apples for her apple pie; she finds them too mushy. Keep in mind that cooking times for apples vary with their hardness.

Pastry for a double-crust 9-inch pie (see Elaine's Pie Crust following)
6 cups sliced Northern Spy apples (Granny Smith, Pippin, and Gravenstein make good substitutes)
¾ cup sugar
1 teaspoon cinnamon
½ teaspoon nutmeg
Scant teaspoon salt
1 teaspoon vanilla
2 tablespoons butter, melted
3 tablespoons flour, plus extra to sprinkle crust
2 to 3 tablespoons Crisco, to brush top crust
2 to 3 tablespoons milk, to brush crust

Following Elaine's Pie Crust recipe (or your own, if you must) line a 9-inch pie plate with pie crust.

Fill to rounding with sliced apples. Add sugar, cinnamon, nutmeg, salt, vanilla, and butter to apples; toss together lightly. Sprinkle flour over all. Cover with top crust. Spread Crisco, several tablespoons of milk, and a sprinkling of flour over top crust, and make vents. Bake in preheated 450°F. oven for 15 minutes. Lower heat to 350° and continue baking 30 more minutes. *Serves 6 to 8.*

ELAINE'S PIE CRUST

Although Elaine rarely bakes pies one at a time, this is her pastry recipe for the basic 9-inch double-crust pie. The recipe traces all the necessary steps for making a pie crust to be proud of. It can be used as is for all the double-crust pies in this segment or divided to use for a single-crust pie.

2 heaping cups all-purpose flour	⅓ to ½ cup iced water as needed
1 teaspoon salt	
2 large mixing spoons Crisco (about ½ cup)	

Blend the flour and salt in a large mixing bowl. Then, using a pastry blender, cut in the shortening until dough forms small pea-sized and still crumbly lumps (this usually takes about 60 quick strokes). Then spoon a hole in the center of the flour-shortening mixture and add ⅓ cup water. With the spoon, fold in the water, adding more if needed, until the dough forms a ball that just holds together when squeezed.

Next, roll out the bottom crust. Lightly flour the board and rolling pin, then spoon out about half the dough, fashioning it into a rounded cake. Next, working from the center, roll out a round crust as thin as possible — about ⅛ inch. (Remember always to work from the center, never back and forth.) When dough is rolled out, carefully drape it in the bottom of the pie plate, pressing it in lightly and trimming off any excess.

When the pie is filled, roll out the second crust in the same manner. When rolled out, spread the crust with a little milk and additional Crisco, and sprinkle it with flour. Cut small vents as needed; then fold crust over and transfer to filled pie. Open up and spread out over the filling evenly, crimping the top and bottom crust edges together. Bake according to pie recipe. When making single-crust shells to be baked and then filled later, prick bottom and sides with a fork before baking.

Makes ample pastry for a double-crust 9-inch pie.

DOUBLE-CRUSTED LEMON PIE

This superb lemon pie is Elaine's former husband's favorite. It is smooth and light, with just the right hint of tartness.

¼ cup cornstarch
¼ cup tap water
1½ cups boiling water
1½ cups sugar
2 tablespoons grated
  lemon rind
1 tablespoon butter
2 eggs, slightly beaten
¼ cup lemon juice
  (about 2 lemons)

Pastry for a double-
  crust 9-inch pie (see
  Elaine's Pie Crust
  above)
1½ to 2 tablespoons
  Crisco, to brush top
  crust
1½ to 2 tablespoons
  milk, to brush crust
Sprinkling of flour, to
  brush top crust

In a medium saucepan, blend cornstarch and tap water. Add boiling water and cook over medium heat, stirring constantly, until thick and clear. Add sugar, lemon rind, and butter. Cool. Stir in eggs and lemon juice (lemons vary in size and juiciness; don't skimp). Turn into unbaked pie shell. Cover with top crust spread with Crisco, milk, and a sprinkling of flour. Make vents. Bake at 425°F. for 10 minutes, then at 375° for 30 minutes. *Serves 6 to 8.*

LEMON MERINGUE PIE

Elaine makes the meringue for this delicious pie in a unique way that enables it to hold up overnight if that should be necessary. Important in her business — but unlikely!

3 eggs	2 cups water
1 cup sugar	2 lemons, grated and
3 tablespoons	juiced
cornstarch	A 9-inch pie shell,
3 tablespoons flour	baked
1 teaspoon salt	

Separate eggs (save whites for meringue). Place beaten yolks, sugar, cornstarch, flour, salt, and water in saucepan. Cook on stove over medium heat, stirring until thick. Remove from stove and add grated lemon rind and juice. Pour into baked pie shell.

MERINGUE:

½ cup water	¼ cup sugar
1 tablespoon cornstarch	3 reserved egg whites
Pinch of salt	½ teaspoon vanilla

Combine all meringue ingredients except for egg whites and vanilla, and cook over medium heat until thick and transparent. Cool completely. While mixture is cooling, beat egg whites until stiff. Then fold egg whites into cooled mixture. Gently beat in vanilla and spread over pie. Bake 10 to 15 minutes at 350°F. until browned.

Serves 6 to 8.

234

CUSTARD PIE

This easy-to-make delicately flavored pie is just right after a heavy meal.

4 eggs	1 teaspoon vanilla
2 cups milk	¼ teaspoon nutmeg
½ cup sugar	A 9-inch pie shell,
Pinch of salt	unbaked

Beat eggs slightly. Add the remaining ingredients and stir well. Pour into an unbaked pie shell. Bake at 450°F. for 10 minutes, then at 300° for 30 minutes. *Serves 8.*

RASPBERRY PIE

What could be better for a refreshing summertime pie than raspberries? Nothing, and this is one of the best.

1 quart fresh raspberries	2 tablespoons butter
A 9-inch pie shell,	1 cup water
baked	3 drops red food
1 cup sugar	coloring (optional)
3 tablespoons	
cornstarch	

Place raspberries into a baked pie shell. Put sugar, cornstarch, butter, and water in pan and cook on stove, stirring constantly, until thickened. Add food coloring, if desired, and pour over raspberries while hot. Cool before serving and offer with a side dish of lightly sweetened whipped cream. *Serves 6 to 8.*

PUMPKIN-WALNUT PIE

This spicy pie has a welcome crunchy texture and makes a nice change from the more traditional baked pumpkin pie.

3 egg yolks, beaten	1 teaspoon vanilla
1 can (15 ounces) pumpkin	1 envelope (1 tablespoon) unflavored gelatin
¾ cup sugar	¼ cup water
½ cup milk	1 cup walnuts, chopped
1 teaspoon cinnamon	A 9-inch pie shell, baked
1 teaspoon nutmeg	
½ teaspoon cloves	1 cup cream, whipped
½ teaspoon salt	

In a saucepan, combine beaten egg yolks, pumpkin, sugar, milk, spices, salt, and vanilla. Bring to a boil, stirring constantly. Remove pan from heat. Dissolve gelatin in the water and add to pan. Stir until smooth. Cool until soupy in texture. Add chopped walnuts. Pour half the mixture into a baked pie shell. Spoon half the whipped cream on top; cover with remaining pumpkin mixture. Decorate top of pie with remaining whipped cream. Allow to cool in refrigerator. *Serves 6 to 8.*

CHOCOLATE CREAM PIE

For chocolate aficionados, this is a wonderful way to get more.

2 cups milk	3 eggs, beaten
⅔ cup sugar	1 teaspoon vanilla
Pinch of salt	A 9-inch pie shell, baked
3 tablespoons cocoa	
2 tablespoons cornstarch	Whipped cream, for garnish

Put milk, sugar, salt, cocoa, and cornstarch in top of a double boiler and cook until slightly thickened, stirring constantly. Add beaten eggs and cook until thick, stirring constantly. Add vanilla and pour into baked pie shell. Let cool, then garnish with whipped cream.

Serves 6 to 8.

MINCE PIE

This tasty mincemeat mixture makes enough filling for close to a dozen pies, but you can make one or more as you want them and refrigerate the unused filling until needed. And although she doesn't add it in her Enterprise pies, Elaine recommends the optional brandy. So, if you like it, by all means put it in.

4 pounds ground beef, gently precooked	2 cups sugar
8 pounds apples, washed, cored, quartered, and run through coarse grinder blade	3 tablespoons ground cinnamon, or more to taste
	2 tablespoons ground nutmeg, or more to taste
2 boxes seedless raisins	1 tablespoon ground cloves, or more to taste
1 box currants	
1 pint brown cider vinegar	1 cup brandy (optional)
1 quart orange juice	Pastry for 9-inch double-crust pies
2 pounds ground suet	
2 cups molasses	

Simmer all ingredients, except pastry, very slowly until cooked (about 2 hours), stirring frequently to prevent sticking. Line pie plate with crust. Add filling (between 2 and 2½ cups per pie). Cover with top crust. Bake at 450°F. for 15 minutes, then at 350° for 30 minutes. *Makes 10 to 12 double-crust 9-inch pies.*

GRASSHOPPER PIE

What a pretty and tasty pie — but how potentially disastrous for the waistline! And what an easy crust! Elaine finds that the Oreo cookie filling is moist enough to hold the crust together without butter.

1½ tablespoons unflavored gelatin	⅓ cup crème de menthe
½ cup sugar	⅓ cup crème de cacao
½ teaspoon salt	1 cup whipping cream
4 eggs, separated	A 9-inch or 10-inch
1 cup water	Oreo Cookie Crust pie shell (see Note below)

Stir and cook together in the top of a double boiler the gelatin, ¼ cup of the sugar, salt, egg yolks, and water until mixture thickens slightly (4 to 5 minutes). Remove from heat. Add crème de menthe and crème de cacao. Chill until consistency of unbeaten egg whites. Beat egg whites until stiff, adding in remaining ¼ cup sugar. Whip cream until stiff. Fold whites and cream together, then fold all ingredients together. Heap into the pie shell and chill until set. (Note: For Oreo Cookie Crust, crush oreo cookies as needed — 18 for the 10-inch, fewer for the 9-inch — and press into pie plate.) *Serves 8 or 10, depending on pie size.*

CHERRY BRANDY PIE

This is a delicious and extremely easy-to-make pie, but very rich.

1 jar (7 ounces)
   marshmallow creme
⅓ cup cherry brandy, or
   less to taste
1 tablespoon cherry
   juice
2½ cups whipping
   cream

2 tablespoons chopped
   cherries
A 9-inch Oreo Cookie
   Crust pie shell (see
   preceding
   Grasshopper Pie)

Combine marshmallow creme and brandy. Beat until smooth. Add cherry juice. Beat whipping cream until stiff. Fold into marshmallow mixture. Fold in cherries and pour into chocolate crust. Freeze overnight. Serve directly from freezer.   *Ample for 8.*

BLACK RUSSIAN PIE

A gourmet pie to end all gourmet pies — the perfect coup de grâce for a very special dinner.

KAHLUA CRUST:

20 chocolate wafers,
   ground fine

¼ cup butter, melted
2 tablespoons Kahlua

Combine ingredients, and press into 9-inch pie plate and cool.

BLACK RUSSIAN FILLING:

⅓ cup Kahlua
2 tablespoons
   unflavored gelatin
½ cup milk
2 eggs, beaten

½ cup sugar
⅔ cup vodka
1½ cups whipping
   cream

Combine Kahlua, gelatin, and milk in a medium-sized saucepan and bring to a boil. Add eggs, sugar, and vodka, mixing gently. Chill until slightly thickened. Whip cream and fold into chilled filling. Pour into pie shell and chill.   *Serves 8.*

Betty Ann Donegan braiding her Danish Christmas wreath.

Visions of Sugarplums

BETTY ANN DONEGAN
Branford, Connecticut

Another culinary thread vital to the weave of New England cookery is that spun around the very special party food that goes so far to help New Englanders mark the celebrations that dot their annual calendar — whether it is to brighten the long upcountry winter days, to welcome the first sparkle of spring, or to help illumine the Independence Day skies.

Whatever the occasion, the person to see is Betty Donegan: party food is her specialty. It is the centerpiece not only for her own parties, but for many of the most successful New Haven (her hometown) fund-raising affairs as well. (More than one person has been overheard to say he or she would give *any* amount to *anything* for a bite of Betty's *spanikopita* — something you can do, by the way, just by trying her recipe here.) Whether it's planning and preparing the classic French dinners put on to benefit the New Haven Symphony, making great stacks of fried dough for Girl Scout jamborees, or creating fanciful birthday cakes for her friends, Betty (who began cooking at age five and studied for a while at the New York Restaurant School) accomplishes it with equal enthusiasm. What's more, she fits it all into a schedule that includes working part-time in her family's New Haven grocery store and overseeing informal cooking classes in her own self-designed double kitchen.

But it is Christmas that inspires Betty to truly prodigal heights. She has been known to bake 40 holiday pies in a single day. Then, too, there are the annual open houses she and her husband, John, host each year to greet their friends (one year it took four separate parties to reach them all). For these, Betty combines the wonderful smells and tastes of cinnamon, cloves, nutmeg, butter, chocolate, and much more, into a splendid array of holiday delights — sugarplums she shares with her friends with a warmth and joy equal to that of any Magus.

CHRISTMAS EGGNOG

Folding the egg whites in at the end makes this well-flavored eggnog frothy and light and just a little bit lumpy, as opposed to the more traditional thicker and smoother nog.

6 eggs, separated	Brandy, whiskey, or
¾ cup sugar	rum, to taste
2 cups heavy cream	Nutmeg, for dusting
2 cups milk	

Beat egg yolks with ½ cup of sugar until lemony. Beat egg whites with the remaining ¼ cup sugar until stiff. Add cream and milk to the yolks and fold in whites. Liquor can be added to the bowl or to cups to taste. Sprinkle generously with nutmeg.

Makes about 1½ quarts.

HOT LOBSTER DIP

This dip is sure to be the hit of any party; the only problem is it disappears too fast.

1 cup mayonnaise	12 ounces lobster or
16 ounces cream cheese,	crabmeat, cut into
softened	small chunks
Dash of garlic powder	Slivered almonds, for
	garnish

Whip mayonnaise together with cream cheese. Add garlic powder and mix well. Rinse lobster meat and pat dry. Fold lobster into mayonnaise mixture and spread thinly in a buttered 7- by 10-inch Pyrex, or similar, pan. Sprinkle with almonds. Bake 30 minutes at 350°F. Serve with crackers or small toast squares.

Makes 4 to 5 cups (30 or 40 servings).

STUFFED MUSHROOMS

Spicy stuffed mushrooms are always a party favorite, and these are yummy. But do remember to keep an eye on them; burnt mushrooms are not so yummy.

1 pound mushrooms	1 egg
1 pound Italian sausage, casing removed	Dash of salt and pepper
¼ cup grated hard cheese	1 cup Italian bread crumbs
1 small onion, grated	Wine, to moisten
1 clove garlic, minced	Olive oil, to drizzle
1 tablespoon chopped parsley	

Select similar-sized mushrooms. Remove stems. Sauté sausage well, breaking into small bits. Cool. Add rest of ingredients, except olive oil. Work mixture with hands until well blended. Fill mushroom caps. Just before baking, drizzle with olive oil. Cover with aluminum foil and bake at 400°F. for 10 minutes (add another 5 to 10 minutes for larger mushrooms). Remove foil and bake 10 more minutes or until they are nicely browned.

Yield: 20 or so, depending on size.

SPANIKOPITA
Spinach Triangles

There are a number of ways to make the filling for this delightful dough-wrapped spinach delicacy — and even several ways to spell it. In fact, in some places the triangles made in this manner are known by a completely different name — tiropitas. Making these may seem a little tricky, but all that's needed is a little practice.

PHYLLO CASING: This recipe is geared to 1 pound phyllo dough and 1 pound unsalted (sweet) butter (melted).

Phyllo dough comes in very, very thin sheets that dry out quickly. It is available in most supermarket freezer cases. When handling this dough, be prepared to work quickly. A good tip is to have a damp tea towel available to cover the dough still in the original roll and also to cover the pieces you're working on should you be interrupted or find yourself working slowly at first. And don't forget to allow time for the dough to thaw out — about 2 hours. If you should have any phyllo sheets left over, they can be refrozen or used with another favorite filling right on the spot.

Remove phyllo sheets from package, 2 at a time. Brush first sheet with butter (a reminder: the butter should be unsalted throughout). Place second sheet on top and brush with butter again. Any part not covered with butter will dry out. Work quickly. Cut each double sheet into four 2-inch-long strips. Place 1 teaspoon of the Spinach Filling (below) about an inch above the bottom of the strip and fold the dough over. Continue to fold dough flag-style. Tuck ends under. Brush both sides with butter. Place on cookie sheet and freeze; *then* place in a plastic bag. If preparing only a few hours ahead, just chill, covered, then bake at 375°F. for 20 to 30 minutes or until golden brown. If frozen, bake about 10 minutes longer. For more triangles, the dough strips can be cut in half horizontally and less filling used.

Yield: 40 or 80, depending on method.

SPINACH FILLING (Recipe for about 1 pound phyllo dough):

¼ cup grated onion
3 tablespoons olive oil
1 package (10 ounces)
  frozen chopped
  spinach, cooked and
  drained
½ teaspoon salt, or less
  to taste

½ teaspoon nutmeg
  (optional)
¼ pound mozzarella
  cheese, grated
½ cup cottage cheese
1 egg

Sauté onion in oil. Add spinach, salt, and nutmeg. Cook slightly. Cool. Mix cheeses together with egg. Stir into spinach mixture.

CRANBERRY-ORANGE BREAD

This is a very tasty and attractive quick bread.

2 cups whole wheat
  flour
2 cups white flour
1 tablespoon baking
  powder
1 teaspoon baking soda
1 teaspoon salt
½ teaspoon cinnamon
¼ teaspoon nutmeg
1 cup firmly packed
  brown sugar

1 cup granulated sugar
½ cup margarine,
  chilled
1 tablespoon finely
  grated orange rind
2 eggs
1½ cups orange juice
2 cups chopped fresh or
  frozen cranberries
1 cup chopped nuts
⅔ cup seedless raisins

Stir together the dry ingredients until well blended. Cut in the margarine with a pastry blender. Combine orange rind with the eggs and orange juice. Mix this liquid into the dry ingredients just until the flour is wet. Fold in the cranberries, nuts, and raisins. Pour into 2 greased and floured 5- by 9-inch loaf pans and bake for 55 to 60 minutes at 350°F. (You can also make 3 medium-sized loaves, 4 small loaves, or 6 tiny loaves; just cook for a shorter time.) Test with a toothpick in the center to see if it comes out clean. Remove from pan and let cool on a wire rack. This bread freezes well and keeps, well wrapped, several days in the refrigerator.

Makes 2 or more loaves.

DANISH CHRISTMAS WREATH

These wreaths are lovely on a holiday party table as well as lovely to eat. They also offer a perfect opportunity to practice your decorating skills. To make the braid as even as possible, Betty works from the center toward the ends.

¾ cup milk	2 packages (scant
½ cup sugar	tablespoon each)
1½ teaspoons salt	active dry yeast
¼ cup plus 1½ cups	3 eggs, beaten, at room
butter (unsalted	temperature
preferred)	4½ cups flour
¼ cup lukewarm water	
(105° to 115° F.)	

Combine milk, sugar, salt, and ¼ cup butter. Scald, then cool to 110°F. Dissolve yeast in water in a large bowl. Add milk mixture, eggs, and 1 cup flour, and beat well. Add rest of flour and mix well. Cover top of dough with greased waxed paper. Chill 2 hours.

Meanwhile, allow 1½ cups butter to soften, then roll it out into about a 10- by 12-inch rectangle between 2 sheets of waxed paper. (If using sticks of butter to do this, cut each stick into fourths lengthwise and lay them out in 3 columns about ½ inch apart.) Place in refrigerator for a few minutes until butter stiffens.

Roll out dough on a floured cloth into a 10- by 20-inch rectangle (approximate). Cover the bottom two-thirds of the dough with chilled butter and fold into thirds, folding the unbuttered third of dough toward the center first. Then turn dough so that the folds are on the sides. Roll out dough again, and again fold into thirds. Wrap loosely in waxed paper, marking the time and the number of turns on a piece of paper, and chill for 1 hour. Roll out *again,* and again fold into thirds and chill. Repeat this process 2 more times. After fourth "turn," chill at least 3 hours, or overnight. As long as dough is well wrapped, it can keep up to 1 week in the refrigerator. Note: When working on this dough, be sure room you are working in is *cold*. If the butter starts to ooze, sprinkle the board with more flour and chill the dough a little longer. Work quickly to keep dough from warming up. When braiding dough, try to keep the seams on the bottom or sides of the braid.

ALMOND FILLING:

8 ounces almond paste	1 egg
¾ cup crushed zwieback	½ teaspoon almond extract
½ cup butter, melted	

Mix ingredients together well until filling is smooth, and set aside, keeping cool.   *Makes enough for 2 wreaths.*

To Assemble Wreath: Roll half of dough into a strip 8 inches by 22 inches and cut into 3 long, straight pieces. Place ⅓ cup of Almond Filling down center of each strip and close edges over filling. Braid the 3 pieces. Form a wreath about 14 inches in diameter and place on brown paper on a cookie sheet. Let rise 1 hour, then bake 30 minutes at 375°F. until golden. Cool on rack and decorate with Confectioners' Sugar Icing (see page 214) and candied fruits. Use egg wash if desired. Repeat process for other half of dough.

Makes 2 wreaths.

FILLING VARIATIONS: Fruit fillings may also be used — raspberry, pineapple, cherry, or blueberry preserves *(not pie filling)* — but use them sparingly. Measure out 1 cup, but if the filling comes too close to the dough edges, use less. Solo filling may also be used, 1 can for 2 wreaths.

COCONUT ISLAND COOKIES

An elegant, tender, fragrant cookie with a lovely not-too-sweet frosting that starts out soft, then forms a light, thin crust when dry. A one-cup container of sour cream divides nicely between the two parts of this cookie.

1 cup firmly packed dark brown sugar	½ teaspoon salt
	½ teaspoon baking soda
¼ pound butter or margarine	Heaping ½ cup sour cream
1 egg	1 cup shredded coconut
3 ounces unsweetened chocolate	1 teaspoon vanilla
	Coconut Island Icing
¼ cup strong coffee	(recipe follows)
2 cups flour	

Cream sugar, butter, and egg. Melt chocolate and coffee together. Cool, add to sugar mixture, and beat well. Add dry ingredients, then sour cream, coconut, and vanilla. Drop by teaspoonfuls onto a greased pan. Bake at 350°F. for 13 minutes. *Do not overbake.* Frost with Coconut Island Icing (below). *Makes 4 dozen 2½-inch cookies.*

COCONUT ISLAND ICING

2 cups confectioners' sugar	2 to 3 tablespoons butter, softened
Scant ½ cup sour cream	1 to 2 teaspoons milk
1 teaspoon vanilla	Coconut, for garnish

Mix all but coconut together and spread on cookies. Sprinkle with shredded coconut.

LINZERTORTE

Very good, very rich, and very professional-looking. A word to the wise: when choosing the preserves for this dessert, pick one without seeds, or run it through a sieve.

1 cup toasted ground
   nuts (almonds or
   hazelnuts)
1½ cups flour
¾ cup sugar
1 teaspoon cinnamon
1 teaspoon baking
   powder
1½ sticks (¾ cup) sweet
   butter

1 egg and 1 egg yolk,
   beaten together
½ cup preserves
   (raspberry,
   strawberry, apricot,
   or your choice)
Confectioners' sugar, for
   dusting

Toast nuts at 400°F. for 10 minutes and chop very fine. Mix together flour, sugar, cinnamon, baking powder, and nuts. Cut in butter and moisten dough with egg, adding only enough to make a pliable but not sticky dough. Wrap in plastic wrap and chill until firm, at least 1 hour. Roll two-thirds of the dough on a flour-covered cloth and line a 9-inch tart pan with removable bottom. Press well into bottom. Spread dough with preserves to within 1 inch of the edge. Roll remaining dough and cut into thin strips. Make a lattice by laying 5 strips (about ½-inch wide) each way. Roll scraps of dough into small ½-inch balls and place them all around inside edge of pan. Bake at 375°F. for 30 minutes (don't let preserves boil). Cool on rack and sprinkle with confectioners' sugar.

Serves 10.

WALNUT BITS

These attractive, crescent-shaped cookies are light and flaky and very easy to prepare. Use several of the fillings suggested to get a fun-to-serve mix of flavors.

½ pound butter, softened	1½ cups flour
½ pound small-curd cottage cheese (sieve if needed)	1 egg
	1 tablespoon cream

Whip butter with cottage cheese until smooth. Add flour to make dough. Chill several hours. Cut dough into thirds. Roll each third into a circle. Cut 8 wedges. Place spoonful of filling (below) on wedge and roll up, bending into crescent shape. Brush with egg mixed with cream. Bake on an ungreased cookie sheet at 350°F. about 20 minutes or until golden.   *Makes 2 dozen.*

FILLING:

1 cup sugar	1 teaspoon cinnamon
1 cup walnuts, chopped	

VARIATION: Any sweet filling may be used — apricot, prune, apple, or your favorite.

BÛCHE DE NOËL

It's not without reason that these lovely, airy yule logs are such a holiday tradition — and this one seems especially divine. It also makes a delicious less-rich treat by omitting the final frosting.

1 cup sifted cake flour	4 eggs, separated
¼ teaspoon salt	1 teaspoon vanilla
1⅓ cups sugar	

Sift the flour with salt and ½ cup sugar. Beat egg whites until foamy, then gradually add ½ cup sugar and beat until stiff. Beat egg yolks with remaining ⅓ cup sugar until lemon-colored. Fold vanilla into egg yolks and then fold egg yolks into egg whites. Finally, fold in flour mixture, 3 tablespoons at a time. Spread evenly in a greased, lined, and regreased 10- by 15-inch jelly-roll pan. Bake at 400°F. for 15 minutes. Turn cake onto a linen towel that has been sprinkled with confectioners' sugar. Remove paper and roll up cake with towel inside. Cool 30 minutes.

FILLING:

1½ cups heavy cream	2 teaspoons instant
½ cup confectioners'	coffee
sugar	1 teaspoon vanilla
¼ cup cocoa	

Combine all ingredients in mixing bowl. Mix well and chill for 15 minutes or so. Beat until thick and chill until needed.

FROSTING:

1 cup semisweet	½ teaspoon vanilla
chocolate chips,	Dash of salt
melted and cooled	1 egg yolk
⅔ cup packed light	½ cup whipping cream,
brown sugar	whipped
3 ounces cream cheese	

Melt chocolate chips in a double boiler. Beat together sugar, cream cheese, vanilla, salt, and egg yolk until smooth and fluffy. Beat in chocolate, then fold in whipped cream. Chill until ready to use, but at least 1 hour.

To Assemble Cake: Unroll cake and spread filling to within 1 inch of edge. Reroll and place on serving dish or wrap in heavy-duty aluminum foil. If cake is being prepared in advance, do not frost until ready to use. Otherwise, spread frosting over whole cake (don't forget ends) and, with a sharp fork, make indentations along entire cake to resemble tree bark. Decorate with red and green candied cherries. (Frosted cake will hold a short while in refrigerator until serving time.) Note: If you prefer not to use frosting, just sprinkle cake liberally with confectioners' sugar and decorate with cherries. *Serves 8 to 10.*

Mary Bevilacqua, front left, and Laurel Gabel, front right, and their fellow cookie exchangers.

The Great Christmas Cookie Exchange

MARY BEVILACQUA and LAUREL GABEL
Wellesley, Massachusetts

There seems no end to the inventive ways in which New Englanders celebrate Christmas. The Annual Great Wellesley Christmas Cookie Exchange — the cookie jar of your dreams — must surely be one of the best.

Ever since the early 1970s, when Mary Bevilacqua and Laurel Gabel, both expert cookie bakers, began this happy tradition, 40 (or more, rarely fewer) cookie-laden Wellesley women have gathered at Mary's candlelit home each December for an evening of early Christmas cheer, good food, and an exchange of their treasured Christmas cookie delights and recipes.

First, Mary and Laurel serve punch and a choice of sumptuous desserts (partly in hope, no doubt, that every cookie won't be gobbled up before their guests leave the premises). Then, when everyone has had her fill, it's on to the serious business at hand. Each guest passes a cookie offering (usually three dozen or so of her most special holiday cookie — anything from kifli to lemon meltaways to gingerbread boys to chocolate mint sticks). From these piles of temptation, each guest selects her own sampling, tucking it away into a personal "cookie jar" to take on home at the end of the evening. (You can tell the hard-core exchangers by the plastic sandwich bags they tote along to ensure that the delicate flavors won't mingle too much.)

Mary and Laurel's cookie exchange idea was most certainly one born for glory. When *Yankee* Magazine published a story on it several years ago offering a sampling of the cookie recipes to all comers, more than 18,000 requests were received within the first three weeks.

Although Mary and Laurel love baking cookies (and share here some of the cookie-making tips they have gathered over the years), they enjoy cooking of all sorts. For a while, they even ran cooking classes for ten students at a time in Mary's kitchen. "We lost money," Mary comments somewhat ruefully, "but we had a good time." In addition, after years of culling and testing recipes, the duo published a cookbook, *A Collection of Holiday Favorites* (a great favorite with their fellow cookie-exchangers and still available for $6.50, plus $1.50 for handling, from Mary, 10 Wall Street, Wellesley, MA 02181).

The Great Christmas Cookie Exchange has so cemented Mary and Laurel's already close friendship that Laurel, now living away from Wellesley, still returns for at least that one December day and evening each year to share again, at least one more time, the annual festivities with Mary and their many friends.

A sampling of the desserts served on that convivial evening, as well as a few of the cookie recipes, follow. Enjoy!

CHRISTMAS PUNCH

This punch is not only pretty — especially welcome for a holiday party — but flavorful as well. A very good nonalcoholic punch. Make plenty — it'll go fast.

1 quart cranberry juice	½ teaspoon almond
1 cup sugar	extract
2 cups orange juice	2 cups ginger ale,
1 cup pineapple juice	chilled
¾ cup fresh or frozen	1 pint pineapple sherbet
lemon juice	

Blend cranberry juice, sugar, fruit juices, and almond extract. Refrigerate, covered, until serving time. Just before serving, stir in ginger ale and sherbet. *Makes 12 eight-ounce cups; 15 six-ounce.*

CIDER WASSAIL

A wonderful cold-weather get-together drink, perfect for a special party or for a more informal après ski. The combination is more flavorful, and with the whipped cream topping, even smoother than the more usual hot buttered rum. Remember when planning bigger batches that whipping cream doubles in volume when whipped.

4 cups good fresh cider
¼ to ⅓ cup dark brown
   sugar
½ cup dark rum
2 tablespoons brandy
2 tablespoons apple
   brandy
1 tablespoon orange
   liqueur
¼ teaspoon cinnamon
¼ teaspoon ground
   cloves
⅛ teaspoon ground
   allspice

Pinch of salt
1 rounded teaspoon
   orange juice
   concentrate
½ cup whipping cream,
   whipped and lightly
   sweetened with 1
   tablespoon
   confectioners' sugar,
   more or less
Fresh nutmeg, for
   garnish (optional)

Bring cider to boil. Add sugar and stir until dissolved. Remove from heat. Stir in rum, brandy, apple brandy, orange liqueur, spices, and salt. Stir in orange juice concentrate. Heat over moderate heat, stirring, for 2 minutes. Pour into demitasse cups or wine glasses and top with a generous dollop of sweetened whipped cream. (The whipped cream makes a big difference in the finished taste of the drink — don't omit it.) Garnish with fresh nutmeg if desired. *Makes enough for 10 to 15 demitasse cupfuls.*

LEMON-ORANGE ANGEL DESSERT

Delicious . . . rich . . . tart . . . creamy . . . and easy to make! If you prefer things a little less rich, you can skip the final whipped cream topping; the pudding is lovely even without it.

1 tablespoon unflavored gelatin	1 angel cake, cubed
4 tablespoons cold water	2 cups medium cream, divided
1 cup boiling water	¼ cup slivered nuts (almonds or other; optional)
¾ cup sugar	
Dash of salt	Shredded coconut (about ¼ cup; optional)
1 cup orange juice	
½ cup lemon juice	
Rind of 1 lemon, grated	

Soften gelatin in cold water. Add boiling water, sugar, and salt; stir. Add juices and rind and stir again. Refrigerate 2 to 3 hours or until slightly jelled and the consistency of unbeaten egg whites. Break cake into small pieces and set aside. Whip 1 cup of cream and fold into gelatin mixture. Line a 2-quart bowl with waxed paper. In lined bowl, put layer of cream mixture and layer of cake cubes. Repeat, ending with cream mixture. Refrigerate 8 hours or overnight. Invert onto cake plate, peel off paper, and frost with remaining whipped cream. Sprinkle with nuts and coconut if desired.

Serves 8 to 10.

BEST CHEESECAKE

No dessert party worth mentioning is without a delicious cheesecake. This is it!

CRUST:

1½ cups graham cracker crumbs	½ teaspoon cinnamon
3 tablespoons sugar	¼ cup sweet butter, melted

FILLING:

3 packages (8 ounces each) cream cheese, at room temperature	2 cups sour cream
	⅓ cup flour
	2 teaspoons vanilla
1¼ cups sugar	Rind of 1 lemon, grated
6 eggs, separated	Juice of ½ lemon

To Prepare Crust: Generously grease a 9-inch spring-form pan with butter. Place pan in center of a 12-inch square of aluminum foil and press foil up around side of pan (foil is to catch any drips). Combine graham cracker crumbs, sugar, cinnamon, and melted butter in a small bowl until well blended. Press ¾ cup of crumb mixture into bottom and sides of pan to make shell. Chill prepared pan while making filling. (Reserve remaining crumb mixture for topping.)

To Add Filling and Complete Cake: Using an electric mixer at low speed, beat cream cheese until soft. Gradually beat in sugar until light and fluffy. Beat in egg yolks, one at a time, until well blended. Stir in sour cream, flour, vanilla, lemon rind, and lemon juice until smooth. Beat egg whites until they hold stiff peaks. Gently fold whites into cheese mixture until well blended. Pour into prepared pan. Top with reserved crumb mixture. Bake at 350°F. for 1¼ hours. Turn the oven off and allow cake to cool in still closed oven for 1 hour. Remove to wire rack and cool to room temperature. Chill overnight before serving. *Serves 10 to 12.*

CHRISTMAS PLUM PUDDING

This fabulously light yet moist pudding is a happy change from the often suety and heavy holiday puddings. It's nice, too, to have a recipe that doesn't have to be made way ahead.

Granulated sugar, for
  dusting mold
½ cup sifted flour
½ teaspoon baking soda
1 teaspoon cinnamon
½ teaspoon ground
  cloves
¼ teaspoon salt
¾ cup fine dry bread
  crumbs
½ cup butter
¾ cup packed light
  brown sugar
3 eggs

1 can (1 pound 14
  ounces) purple
  plums, drained and
  chopped
1 tablespoon freshly
  grated orange rind
8 ounces pitted dates,
  chopped
1 cup seedless raisins
8 ounces mixed candied
  fruits, chopped
1 cup chopped pecans
½ cup currants
Plum Pudding Rum
  Sauce (recipe follows)

Grease an 8-cup pudding mold and dust evenly with granulated sugar. Sift flour, soda, cinnamon, cloves, and salt into a small bowl. Stir in bread crumbs. Set aside. Cream butter and brown sugar, then beat in the eggs, one at a time. Stir in plums and orange rind. Gently blend in the flour mixture, then fold in dates, raisins, candied fruit, pecans, and currants. Spoon into prepared mold. Lock mold lid in place or cover with foil and tie tightly with string. Place on a rack in a kettle that has a tight-fitting lid. Pour in boiling water to about half the depth of the mold. Cover tightly and steam over low heat for about 4½ hours or until pudding is firm. Cool pudding in mold for 5 minutes. Loosen around edge with knife. Invert onto serving plate. Allow to stand at least 15 minutes to cool. Serve warm with Plum Pudding Rum Sauce. Pudding may be made ahead and frozen. To warm for serving, defrost pudding, wrap in foil, and heat in a 400°F. oven for 30 minutes.

Yield: 16 to 20 small servings.

PLUM PUDDING RUM SAUCE

A sauce that one taster tagged "pure nectar." It's hard to imagine that anyone would disagree.

3 ounces cream cheese
1 egg
1 cup confectioners' sugar
2 tablespoons butter
1 teaspoon lemon juice
Pinch of salt
1 cup heavy cream, whipped
2 tablespoons golden rum, more or less to taste

Beat cheese until light. Add egg, sugar, butter, lemon juice, and salt. Beat well. Fold in whipped cream and rum to taste just until combined. Store, covered, in the refrigerator. *Makes 2 cups.*

MARY AND LAUREL'S COOKIE-BAKING TIPS

• Always use unsalted butter — it gives cookies a lighter texture.

• After cutting or shaping cookies, put them on cookie sheets and slip them into the freezer for a few minutes to help them hold their shape when they are baked. This also seems to make the cookies flakier.

• If cookie dough is too sticky, chill it rather than add more flour. Too much flour makes cookies dry.

• Always use a pastry cloth when rolling out ginger-bread boys and other cutout cookies — it reduces problems with sticky dough.

• Be sure your cookie tins are flat, not warped, so that cookies will bake uniformly. Turn the tins at least once during baking.

• Use a flour sifter to dust confectioners' sugar onto cookies.

• Let cookie sheets cool off between batches — a hot cookie sheet will make dough start to melt.

• When freezing cookies, place waxed paper between layers, and use good airtight containers — you can reuse the waxed paper and the containers.

• Buy expensive ingredients like walnuts and coconut when they are on sale and store them in the freezer.

LAUREL'S KIFLI

These cookies resemble a mock almond-filled puff pastry and are a delicious addition to the holiday cookie jar.

DOUGH:

2 cups flour	2 egg yolks, slightly
1 cup butter	beaten
	½ cup sour cream

FILLING:

10 ounces walnuts, ground (about 2 cups)	1½ teaspoons almond extract
½ cup granulated sugar	1 egg, beaten with a
¼ cup light cream or milk	little water

To Make Dough: Cut butter into flour with a pastry blender until mixture resembles coarse crumbs. Add egg yolks and sour cream; stir until just combined. Knead briefly on a lightly floured surface until dough is smooth. Shape into a flat round, wrap in plastic wrap, and refrigerate.

To Make Filling: Combine nuts, sugar, milk, and almond extract. Blend well.

Preheat oven to 400°F. Grease cookie sheets. On a lightly floured surface, roll out half of the dough until it is about ⅛-inch thick, shaped roughly 12 inches by 16 inches. Cut into 2-inch squares. Use a soft paintbrush to paint the top of each square lightly with the egg-water wash. Spread a rounded half teaspoonful of filling diagonally down center of square. Bring 2 opposite corners up to overlap; pinch to seal. Repeat whole process with the other half of the dough. Brush tops of all with egg-water mixture and sprinkle lightly with sugar. Place about 2 inches apart on a greased cookie sheet. Bake until nicely browned, about 10 to 15 minutes. Cool on rack. Dust with confectioners' sugar.

Makes about 5 to 6 dozen cookies.

CHOCOLATE MINT STICKS

There's hardly a better flavor blend than chocolate and mint, and this prettily dolled-up confection has plenty of both. The base for this cookie is almost fudglike, though not as sweet.

2 beaten eggs
½ cup margarine,
  melted
2 squares (1 ounce each)
  unsweetened
  chocolate, melted

1 cup sugar
½ teaspoon vanilla
½ cup flour

FROSTING:

2 tablespoons butter
1 cup sifted
  confectioners' sugar
1 tablespoon cream
½ teaspoon peppermint
  flavoring or 1 to 2
  tablespoons crème de
  menthe thickened
  with a little
  confectioners' sugar

½ (½ ounce) square
  unsweetened
  chocolate, melted
1½ tablespoons butter,
  melted

To Make Cookies: Combine all ingredients except flour; beat well. Blend in flour. Pour into a greased and floured 9-inch square pan. Bake at 350°F. for 25 minutes. Cool.

To Add Frosting: Mix butter, sugar, cream, and mint flavoring. Spread over cooled baked layer. When frosting is firm, mix melted chocolate and butter, and drizzle over all. Place in refrigerator until firm. Cut into small sticks or squares and put in small cupcake papers. *Makes about 4½ dozen.*

MARY'S LEMON-NUTMEG MELTAWAYS

A light and simple cookie with a hint of nutmeg and lemon. A tangy counterpoint to the frequently richer holiday sweet.

1 cup sifted cake flour
½ cup cornstarch
¼ teaspoon salt
½ teaspoon nutmeg
10 tablespoons unsalted
    butter, softened

½ cup confectioners'
    sugar, plus extra for
    ringing cutter
2 teaspoons grated
    lemon rind

Sift dry ingredients onto waxed paper. Beat butter, sugar, and lemon rind in mixer until light and fluffy. Add dry ingredients. Beat on low speed until mixture is smooth. Shape teaspoonfuls of dough into balls and place on an ungreased baking sheet. Flatten slightly to 1¼-inch circles with the bottom of a glass dipped in confectioners' sugar. Bake at 325°F. for 15 minutes or until golden brown around the edges. Cool for 2 minutes on cookie sheet and then transfer to a wire rack to finish cooling.

Makes approximately 3 dozen.

Pocomoonshine Cakewalk originator Jane Dudley (seated) and her fellow cake bakers, Ethel Wallace (on left) and Ellie Sanford (with her daughter Emily), enjoying an early view of only some of the prize cakes to go to lucky cakewalkers.

The Pocomoonshine
Chocolate Cakewalk

JANE DUDLEY and FELLOW MEMBERS
Alexander-Crawford Historical Society, Maine

You have to dance for dessert at this innovative New England fund-raising party. Ever since 1980, one night a year (originally the night of the Historical Society's annual meeting; more recently, the Fourth of July), the society's members (an astounding 400 from a combined community of little more than 500), gather for an evening of dancing, refreshments, and a much-anticipated chocolate cakewalk.

The big moment comes when the cakewalkers parade around the room to an upbeat talking-blues tune especially composed and recorded for the occasion — until, when the music stops, the lucky walkers left standing on cake symbols imprinted on the floor get a chance to pick (for a fee) from the long table holding the best chocolate cakes in both towns.

Faced with the need to raise funds for the Historical Society and haunted by the memory of church suppers where, years back, bidders for dessert cakes had to follow a string to their prize, it was no accident that the thoughts of Jane Dudley, founder and then president, turned to chocolate cake and then to an annual cakewalk. What better way for the society to raise the funds needed to help preserve the history of that pine woods and blueberry barrens Washington County area? There was no lack of local culinary talent and surely no lack of appetite.

And Jane's idea certainly caught on. When the cakewalk (named for the Pocomoonshine Lake site of Jane and her husband

265

Jack's 1910 log cabin — and the historical society's winter meeting headquarters) began, there were 18 cakes selling for $1.00 (!) each. The number of cakes goes up each year — along with the price. Who knows what the year 2000 will bring? If you can't be at the Alexander-Crawford Historical Society annual cakewalk to see for yourself, why not get some friends and use some of the Pocomoonshine Cakewalk recipes to have a cakewalk of your own?

KAREN SEARS'S CHOCOLATE CHEESECAKE

Another pure delight! The texture is a little grainy — as cheesecakes are — but still very light. Use the crust for Refrigerator Cheese Pie on page 184 or for the Best Cheesecake on page 257.

1 cup cottage cheese	2 egg whites, stiffly
½ cup sugar	beaten
½ cup chopped walnuts	1 9- or 10-inch graham
2 egg yolks	cracker shell, baked
1 teaspoon vanilla	(see page 184 or 257)
8 ounces semisweet	Walnut halves and
chocolate, melted	whipped cream, for
1 cup heavy cream,	garnish
whipped	

Combine cottage cheese, sugar, walnuts, egg yolks, and vanilla in a large bowl, and beat with an electric mixer at high speed until smooth. Add melted chocolate. Fold in whipped cream, then fold in egg whites. Place mixture in a baked shell, cover with plastic wrap, and refrigerate for 24 hours. Garnish with walnut halves and extra whipped cream just before serving. Note: If you have extra filling, spoon it into the little paper muffin cups to make petite individual cheesecakes. *Will serve 12 or more.*

CLARICE PERKINS'S
CHOCOLATE CHIFFON CAKE

This light chiffon cake offers a less rich alternative for the Cakewalk prize table. Less rich, perhaps, but every bit as good as its heavier counterparts.

2 eggs, separated	⅓ cup salad oil
1½ cups sugar, divided	1 cup buttermilk
1¾ cups sifted cake flour	2 ounces unsweetened chocolate, melted
¾ teaspoon baking soda	Chocolate Deluxe Icing (recipe follows)
¾ teaspoon salt	

Preheat oven to 350°F. Grease and flour two round 8-inch layer pans or one 9- by 13-inch pan. Beat egg whites until frothy. Gradually beat in ½ cup of the sugar. Continue beating until stiff and glossy; then set aside. Sift remaining sugar, flour, soda, and salt into another bowl. Add oil, and half of the buttermilk, and beat for 1 minute at medium speed or by hand for 150 strokes. Scrape sides and bottom of bowl constantly. Add the remaining ½ cup buttermilk, egg yolks, and chocolate. Beat for 1 minute more, scraping bowl constantly. Fold in set-aside meringue mixture. Pour into prepared pans. Bake layers for 30 to 35 minutes; an oblong cake pan 40 to 45 minutes. Cool. Frost with Chocolate Deluxe Icing.

Serves 8 to 10, or more from the oblong pan.

CHOCOLATE DELUXE ICING

Another choice frosting to gild the chocolate lilies.

2 cups sifted confectioners' sugar	⅓ cup butter, softened
¼ teaspoon salt	2 ounces unsweetened chocolate, melted
1 large egg	

Combine all ingredients; beat until fluffy and spread over cooled cake. *Makes ample for a 2-layer or standard oblong cake.*

JANE GEROW DUDLEY'S
POCOMOONSHINE CHOCOLATE CAKE

When they say chocolate in Alexander and Crawford, Maine, they mean CHOCOLATE — and they also mean good cakes. This one is chocolate top to bottom and delicious all the way.

2 cups cake flour	1½ cups sugar
1 teaspoon baking soda	2 eggs, separated
½ teaspoon salt	¾ cup buttermilk or
½ cup boiling water	sour milk
½ cup unsweetened	1 teaspoon vanilla
cocoa (Baker's	Cabin Chocolate
preferred)	Frosting (recipe
½ cup butter	follows)

Sift cake flour 3 times with baking soda and salt. Add boiling water slowly to the cocoa to make a smooth paste; cool. Cream butter and sugar. Add egg yolks, one at a time, beating well after each addition. Add cocoa mixture. Add dry ingredients alternately with mixture of buttermilk and vanilla, beating well each time. Beat egg whites until they are stiff but not dry and fold into cake mixture. Grease two 9-inch layer pans and line the bottoms with waxed paper. Divide batter between the pans and bake at 350°F. for 30 minutes or until cakes test done. Cool and frost with Cabin Chocolate Frosting. *Makes 10 to 12 servings.*

CABIN CHOCOLATE FROSTING

A rich and creamy yet light-textured chocolate frosting.

3 ounces unsweetened	⅛ teaspoon salt
chocolate	7 tablespoons rich milk
3 tablespoons butter	or cream
3 cups sifted	1 teaspoon vanilla
confectioners' sugar	

Melt the chocolate and butter over hot water, or over very low heat. In a large bowl, blend the sifted confectioners' sugar, salt, milk, and vanilla. Add the hot chocolate mixture and beat well. Let stand, stirring occasionally, until the frosting is of the proper consistency to spread on the cooled cakes. (If frosting is too thin, add more confectioners' sugar.) *Makes ample for a 2-layer cake.*

ELINOR SANFORD'S
SATAN'S VELVET ROBE CAKE

A sumptuous cake! Only an angel could resist such temptation.

1½ teaspoons baking soda, dissolved in ⅓ cup cold water
½ cup butter or margarine
1¾ cups sugar, divided
1 teaspoon salt
1 teaspoon vanilla
½ cup cocoa, stirred into ⅓ cup cold water
2½ cups sifted cake flour
1 cup cold water
3 egg whites, beaten
Emily's Icing (recipe follows)

Combine soda and ⅓ cup water and set aside. Cream butter with 1 cup sugar and beat until fluffy. Blend in salt and vanilla. Add mixture of cocoa and water. Scrape bowl and beaters and mix until cocoa is well blended. Add cake flour alternately with 1 cup cold water; blend in a meringue of the egg whites and remaining ¾ cup sugar. Add mixture of soda and water and mix well. Pour into 2 greased and floured 9-inch round layer pans, or one 9- by 13-inch pan. Bake at 350°F. for about 30 minutes or until cake tests done. Cool, and frost with Emily's Icing.

Makes 12 to 15 good-sized pieces.

EMILY'S ICING

¼ cup butter
3½ cups confectioners' sugar
1½ teaspoons vanilla
½ cup cocoa
¼ teaspooon salt
⅓ cup milk

Combine all ingredients, beating well, and spread over cooled cake.
Makes ample for a 2-layer or large oblong cake.

ELLEN WELLS'S FUDGE CAKE

This fudge cake made with brown sugar is another winner.

1 stick (½ cup) butter	2 cups cake flour or 1¾
1 pound brown sugar	cups all-purpose flour
2 eggs	1½ cups milk
3 squares (1 ounce each)	1 teaspoon vanilla
bitter chocolate,	Chock Full of Chocolate
melted	Frosting (recipe
1 teaspoon baking soda	below)

Cream butter and sugar. Add eggs; beat well. Stir in melted chocolate. Add sifted dry ingredients alternately with milk and vanilla mixture, beginning and ending with dry ingredients. Pour batter into 2 greased and floured 9-inch pans. Bake at 350°F. for about 40 minutes, until cake tests done. When cake is cool, frost with icing. *Makes 8 to 10 slices.*

CHOCK FULL OF CHOCOLATE FROSTING

If this doesn't set chocolate lovers' teeth to aching, we don't know what will.

3 squares (1 ounce each)	1 tablespoon corn syrup
unsweetened baking	1 cup sugar
chocolate	1 egg, lightly beaten
1 cup heavy cream	1 teaspoon vanilla

Combine the chocolate, cream, corn syrup, and sugar in a small heavy saucepan. Over low flame, heat, stirring, until the chocolate is melted and the sugar is dissolved. Raise heat to medium and, stirring only enough to prevent sticking, cook until the mixture reaches 224° to 226°F. on a candy thermometer or forms a soft ball when dropped into water. Then, using a small wire whisk, beat the hot mixture into the egg. Cool to room temperature and stir in the vanilla. *Makes ample for a double-layer 9-inch cake.*

MARIAN COUSINS'S SAUERKRAUT CAKE

The sauerkraut gives this pleasantly moist cake a slightly crunchy texture similar to coconut, but without any noticeable sauerkraut taste.

⅔ cup butter
1¼ cups sugar
3 eggs
1 teaspoon vanilla
½ rounded cup cocoa
2¼ cups flour
1 teaspoon baking soda

¼ teaspoon salt
1 cup water
⅔ cup drained
   sauerkraut
Cream Cheese Frosting
   (recipe follows)

Cream butter and sugar until fluffy. Add eggs one at a time; add vanilla and mix well. Sift dry ingredients together and add to egg mixture alternately with the water. Add the sauerkraut and mix well. Bake in greased 8-inch layer pans or in a 9- by 13-inch pan at 350°F. for 30 to 40 minutes or until cake tests done. Frost with Cream Cheese Frosting or another of your choice.

Serves 8 to 10, or more from the oblong pan.

CREAM CHEESE FROSTING

A mildly flavored frosting that allows the cake flavor to shine through.

3 ounces cream cheese,
   softened
1 pound confectioners'
   sugar

3 teaspoons vanilla
3 to 4 tablespoons milk
   as needed
Pinch of salt

Beat cream cheese at medium speed until smooth. Gradually add sugar, vanilla, and as much milk as needed to make a spreadable mix. Add a pinch of salt and beat for at least 5 minutes. Be sure cake is thoroughly cooled before frosting. When frosted, refrigerate cake about 15 minutes to set frosting.

Ample for 8-inch double-layer or standard oblong cake.

KATHRYN SMITH'S BUTTERCREAM FROSTING

Another vanilla frosting — this one a buttercream. It has nice flavor and spreads easily.

6 tablespoons butter or margarine, softened	1 pound confectioners' sugar
1 teaspoon vanilla	3 to 4 tablespoons milk
⅛ teaspoon salt	

Cream butter with vanilla. Add salt. Gradually add confectioners' sugar, beating thoroughly after each addition. Stir in milk and beat until frosting is the right consistency for spreading.

Makes enough for two 9-inch layers or 3 dozen cupcakes.

ALBERTA JAMES'S CHOCOLATE CREAM FROSTING

A superior and finely textured chocolate frosting. If you're left with any extra, it makes a good "fudge" just as is.

3 ounces cream cheese	⅛ teaspoon salt
¼ cup milk	1 teaspoon vanilla
3 cups sifted confectioners' sugar	3 ounces unsweetened chocolate, melted

Blend cream cheese with the milk. Add confectioners' sugar, salt, and vanilla. Beat in the chocolate, stirring until mixture is smooth.

Ample for a 2-layer or large oblong cake.

ETHEL WALLACE'S
WHITE MOUNTAIN FROSTING

Just how this vanilla frosting snuck in among all this delicious chocolate we don't know, but it's a mighty good one.

2 cups sugar	¾ cup water
¼ teaspoon cream of tartar	2 egg whites
	1 teaspoon vanilla

Mix sugar, cream of tartar, and water in a saucepan. Boil slowly, without stirring, until mixture spins a 6-inch to 8-inch thread when a little is dropped from a spoon held over the saucepan. Keep the pan covered for the first 3 minutes to prevent crystals from forming on the sides of the pan. While syrup is cooking, beat egg whites until stiff enough to hold a peak. Pour the hot syrup very slowly in a thin stream into the egg whites, beating constantly. Add vanilla and continue beating until mixture is fluffy and will hold its shape.   *Ample to frost a 2-layer or standard oblong cake.*

Patricia Dunlea adds a little "style" to her roast chicken.

Sunday Dinner . . . With Style

PATRICIA DUNLEA
Wellesley Hills, Massachusetts

As all New England cooks strive to make their food and its trappings as attractive and welcoming as possible, so does Pat Dunlea. However, for Pat, this effort does double duty; at home for her son, Jack, and daughter, Jennifer, and for her career as food stylist working on some of the biggest food accounts in the Boston area.

Trained as a home economist at Regis College in nearby Weston, Pat planned to teach, until a college internship led her to food styling instead. Her first job found her at work as a demonstrator for Boston Electric, but it wasn't long before she was hosting their *Electric Living* TV show, when shows were live and when gelatin salads that didn't jell didn't jell for the whole world to see. Work in advertising and as the first full-time photography-studio food stylist in the area followed, until, for a spell, Pat took time out to start her family.

Today, Pat is again doing much the same work but on a freelance basis. Her work is varied, never the same from one day to the next, which, as she readily admits, is "one of the reasons I like it so much." But it isn't easy. One day may find her mounting a multicolored ice-cream-scoop-mountain display for the Friendly Restaurant chain's summer menu cover (working with ice cream, she says, is the hardest thing she has to do; the hot lights melt it so quickly). The next day, she may have to pull off a minor miracle — saving the day when a household dog eats the biscuits vital to that morning's shoot. And the next may find her pushing hard to meet the editorial deadline for her quarterly food feature in *Gray's Sporting Journal*.

It was her expertise with food and her work as a food stylist that led the Yankee Books editors to ask Pat to plan, prepare, and style the food for the *More Great New England Recipes* book jacket. She was asked to work up something with a delicious New England flavor. Her first thought was a natural: a stylish Sunday dinner — both traditional and special. She then planned the menu you see on the jacket, wrote out the recipes, and prepared and arranged the food for the cover shoot.

However, the food on Pat's photo dinner party table is not always what it seems. The chicken has been roasted only 20 to 30 minutes so it won't pucker under the hot lights (she can roast it more later to eat if she wants), the gravy is colored yogurt (easier and faster than the real thing), the vegetables around the roast have been oiled so they'll shine (Pat never uses anything inedible for her "touch up" work), and the pepper (in short supply) is slanted ski-slope style (away from the camera) in its crystal shaker in order to show up for the shot. Fortunately, the dog has been put out, so the biscuits should stay intact.

But don't be fooled twice: the recipes behind Pat's chicken dinner party menu are bona fide — and delicious. Pat has developed her fine recipes over her many years of working with food, and she never stops honing them closer and closer to perfection. Trust us and try them; you won't be sorry.

ROLLED STUFFED FISH FILLETS

Although these delicate fish rolls are part of this dinner party menu as an appetizer cut into one-inch pieces, they also make a lovely light main dish served as is.

4 skinless, boneless fillets of sole or flounder (approximately 8 inches by 4 or 5 inches and all the same size)	½ cup wheat cracker crumbs
	2 tablespoons chopped parsley
	6 tablespoons butter, melted
1 cup soft bread crumbs	2 tablespoons dry sherry

Preheat oven to 400°F. Place fillets, skinned-side up, on a flat surface. Combine the bread and cracker crumbs with parsley, 3 tablespoons melted butter, and 1 tablespoon sherry. Toss gently. Center equal portions of the filling on top of the fillets and spread evenly, leaving a slight margin on all sides. Roll up each fillet and secure with a long toothpick or skewer. Put the remaining 3 tablespoons of the butter and 1 tablespoon of the sherry in a shallow baking dish and place in oven for several minutes until hot. Place fish rolls in the baking dish and baste with butter-sherry sauce. Bake for 15 minutes, turning once with tongs. If difficult to manipulate, skip the turning (it's not absolutely necessary). To serve as an appetizer, slice into 1-inch pieces and serve on a leaf of romaine lettuce with a wedge of lemon.

Ample appetizers for 6; serves 4 as a main dish.

LOBSTER BISQUE

A simply sensational and very pretty bisque! A lobster could hardly hope to meet a more glorious end. But it's so rich, with a full dinner you'll want only a little.

¼ cup butter or
    margarine
¼ cup minced onion
¼ cup minced carrot
3 plum tomatoes,
    peeled and chopped
1 pound lobster meat,
    chopped
⅓ cup dry white wine
2 cups fish stock or
    water

2 cups all-purpose
    cream
2 egg yolks, lightly
    beaten
1 teaspoon fresh thyme
    or scant ¼ teaspoon
    dried
Salt to taste
Pinch of white pepper
3 tablespoons brandy
    (optional)

In a heavy saucepan, melt butter and cook onion, carrot, and all but ¼ cup tomatoes over low heat for 5 minutes. Add all but ½ cup of the lobster meat and quickly sauté for several minutes. Add wine and fish stock or water, cover, and simmer for 10 minutes. Remove from heat and let stand for up to 1 hour to allow flavors to blend. Purée mixture in an electric blender a little at a time. Pour into top of a double boiler over simmering water. Stir in cream and heat for about 5 minutes. Pour a small amount of hot mixture into beaten egg yolks, return to pan, stirring constantly, and heat while stirring until slightly thickened. Add seasonings and brandy, if desired. At serving time, garnish with reserved tomatoes and lobster meat. *Serves 6.*

HERBED VINAIGRETTE SAUCE FOR SALAD

The combination of garlic, wine vinegar, and tarragon makes an excellent zesty dressing for greens of all sorts and particularly for Boston lettuce.

½ cup olive oil
½ teaspoon salt
1 clove garlic, crushed
1 teaspoon tarragon (optional)
1 teaspoon Dijon mustard
1 teaspoon parsley

2 to 3 tablespoons wine vinegar or lemon juice
Boston lettuce, torn into bite-sized pieces
½ cup croutons, more or less

Combine olive oil with seasonings, mustard, and parsley, and gradually beat in the vinegar, tasting as you add to determine the proper proportions. Wash and dry lettuce. Toss lettuce with dressing and sprinkle on croutons.   *Makes about ¾ cup.*

ROAST CHICKEN
WITH BREAD AND SAUSAGE STUFFING

A lovely roast chicken with a moist, fluffy, and perfectly seasoned stuffing. The bacon slices add just a hint of smoke, and the glaze, if you use it, a hint of sweet. A real winner!

1 roasting chicken (4 to 6 pounds)	⅛ teaspoon thyme
½ lemon	⅛ teaspoon marjoram
Salt as needed	1 tablespoon minced parsley
½ pound sausage meat	1 egg, lightly beaten
¼ cup minced onion	3 slices bacon
¼ cup thinly sliced celery	½ cup cider (optional)
2 cups fresh bread cubes	2 tablespoons brown sugar
⅛ teaspoon sage	

Remove chicken giblets, liver, and other parts, and wash bird; pat dry. Rub interior with the lemon. Then sprinkle neck and body cavity with salt.

To Make Stuffing: Cook sausage meat in a skillet for 10 minutes or until done. Remove with a slotted spoon and drain. Pour off all but 2 tablespoons of drippings, then stir-fry the onions and celery for about 5 minutes. Combine with the bread cubes, herbs, parsley, and beaten egg and mix well.

To Stuff and Roast Chicken: Loosely fill bird with stuffing. Skewer or sew openings shut and truss by folding wings back and under body and tying legs close to body so the bird will roast more evenly. Place bird in a shallow roasting pan and arrange bacon slices over top of chicken. Cook in a preheated 325°F. oven 20 to 25 minutes per pound, basting often with pan juices, about 2 to 2½ hours.

When bacon is crisp or during last 30 minutes of cooking (whichever is sooner), remove bacon. Then, if desired, brush with a glaze of the cider and brown sugar, which have been cooked to blend.

To test for doneness, cover thumb and forefinger with a bit of paper towel and pinch the thickest part of the thigh; if the meat feels very soft, the bird is done. (Another method of testing the roast is to prick it with a fork: if the juices run clear, it's done. Pat prefers that there be a few drops of pink juice along with the clear; she finds that leaves the breast meat moister.)

After removing bird from oven, allow to stand for 10 to 15 minutes before carving. Serve with pan gravy and the Spiced Cranberry-Peach Sauce following.   *Ample for 6.*

SPICED CRANBERRY-PEACH SAUCE

The peaches and cranberries in this recipe combine to add a lovely bit of color to a dinner party table, and spicy good taste as well.

1 can (16 ounces) Cling peach slices	1 teaspoon whole cloves
	1 cinnamon stick
1 cup sugar	2 cups fresh cranberries
¼ cup raspberry vinegar	

Drain peaches, reserving ¾ cup of the syrup. Combine the reserved syrup, sugar, and vinegar in a saucepan. Make a bouquet garni (little cheesecloth bag) of cloves and cinnamon stick and add to saucepan. Bring to a boil. Remove spices and add cranberries to peach mixture. Again bring to boil. Cook without stirring over medium-high heat for about 5 minutes or until skins pop. Remove from heat and add peaches. Cool and keep covered in refrigerator until ready to serve.   *Makes 2 to 3 cups.*

MAPLE SUGAR BISCUITS

A classic biscuit laced with maple sugar. A welcome bit of New England for this dinner menu and also for breakfast.

2 cups flour	¾ cup milk
3 teaspoons baking powder	2 to 3 tablespoons butter, melted
½ teaspoon salt	½ cup crushed maple sugar
¼ cup shortening	

Sift dry ingredients into a bowl. Cut in shortening. Add milk to make a soft dough. Place on a floured board and toss lightly. Roll out to ½-inch thick and cut with floured biscuit cutter. Place on a greased cookie sheet. Brush tops of biscuits with melted butter and sprinkle with maple sugar. Bake in a 450°F. oven for 10 to 12 minutes. *Makes 12 biscuits.*

DATE AND NUT BREAD

A nice taste and color contrast for this dinner party's bread basket. May also be made into two smaller loaves, one to serve and one to save.

8 ounces pitted dates, chopped	2 cups sugar
1½ cups boiling water	1 egg, beaten
2 teaspoons baking soda	2¾ cups flour
1 tablespoon butter, melted	½ teaspoon salt
	1 cup chopped walnuts

Combine dates, boiling water, and baking soda in a large heatproof bowl. When mixture is cool, add the melted butter and stir in the sugar thoroughly. Add the egg and blend well. Sift together flour and salt and carefully stir into date mixture. When thoroughly blended, fold in nuts. Place in a well-greased large 5- by 9-inch loaf pan or two smaller pans. Bake in a preheated 350°F. oven for about 70 minutes (the smaller pans will take less time). The bread is done when a cake tester inserted in the center comes out clean — watch so that it doesn't become overly browned. Good sliced thin as is or spread with cream cheese. *Makes 1 or 2 loaves, depending on size.*

ORANGE-RICE PUDDING

An ordinary pudding made very special by the addition of orange-flavored liqueur and zest — and presented oh, so prettily. A lovely light end to a full dinner.

2 cups milk, scalded	½ cup plumped raisins
½ cup sugar	1 teaspoon slivered
Pinch of salt	orange zest
2 large eggs, separated	1 orange, rind removed,
1 cup cooked rice	sliced and halved
1 tablespoon Grand	Pouring or whipped
Marnier or Cointreau	cream

Heat milk, sugar, and salt in top of a double boiler. Cook until sugar is dissolved. Pour a little hot mixture into the lightly beaten egg yolks; beat thoroughly, then return to hot milk mixture. Cook until thickened, stirring constantly. Add rice, liqueur, raisins, and orange zest. Blend well and cool. Beat the egg whites until stiff and fold into the rice mixture. Arrange orange slices artistically in serving bowl, and spoon in pudding. Serve with pouring or whipped cream. *Serves 6 to 8.*

An Index

285